Succeeding When You're Supposed to Fail

Succeeding When You're Supposed to Fail

THE 6 ENDURING PRINCIPLES

OF HIGH ACHIEVEMENT

Rom Brafman

THREE RIVERS PRESS

NEW YORK

Library of Congress Cataloging-in-Publication Data
Brafman, Rom.
Succeeding when you're supposed to fail : the 6 enduring principles of high
achievement / Rom Brafman.
Includes bibliographical references.
1. Success. 2. Success in business. I. Title.
BF637.S8B67 2012
158—dc23
2011023816

ISBN 978-0-307-88769-6
eISBN 978-0-307-88770-2

Printed in the United States of America

Book design by Leonard Henderson
Cover design by Alison Forner
Author photograph: © Josyn Herce

10 9 8 7 6 5 4 3 2 1

First Paperback Edition

To Josyn, Ori, Tsilla, and Hagay

Contents

Succeeding When You're Supposed to Fail

Prologue

There's something I find fascinating about other people's professions. What is it *really* like to be a football coach? Or a paleontologist? Or a zookeeper? Luckily, in my work as a psychologist and an author, I get to learn about many of these worlds. A few months ago, I was talking with an emergency medical technician (they don't like to be called ambulance drivers) who shared with me his pet peeve: motorists who routinely cut him off. "Just because my sirens and lights are not on," he explains with resigned frustration, "doesn't mean I don't have a patient in the back."

Sometimes the insights I gain are more significant. After the financial markets collapse of 2008, I interviewed an investment banker who related his observations about the banking industry. What surprised him most was the degree to which popularity played a role in shaping investment decisions. "It's just like high school," he lamented. "If you're part of the in-crowd then your suggestions will be taken seriously, even if the facts and figures don't support them." And if you're not, any alarm bells you sound will get politely ignored. This type of high school culture, he believed, led to poor investment choices that helped to set the stage for the financial meltdown.

As much as I enjoy learning about other fields, though, my true passion is the discipline of psychology. The field is still relatively young; there are still many questions left unanswered about the way our mind works. But enough research has been conducted to give us meaningful insights into some of the ways our mind functions and why we behave the way we do. I believe that today we are on the cusp of learning more about ourselves than we ever knew before.

One of the most profound insights I've learned from psychology is that there doesn't seem to be a limit to the power of the human spirit to bounce back from setbacks and adversity. As a therapist, I've worked with individuals who have experienced incredible hardships but have still found a way to overcome them. Somehow they managed to persevere against the odds, altering the path that life seemed to have in store for them. This ability to be successful despite adversity is one of the most intriguing aspects about the human psyche. And up until recently psychologists knew very little about it.

The prevailing notion in the field used to be that few could realistically overcome their circumstances. And because psychologists focused so much of their attention on trying to understand pathology, they overlooked the most positive and inspiring accounts of individuals who overcame the odds and demonstrated surprising resilience.

The field changed course completely by accident. While conducting longitudinal studies, researchers came across large groups of individuals who appeared to defy the classical psychological dogma about the overbearing effects of adversity. And, as it turns out, people who overcome adversity are more common than psychologists thought. As the field broadened its horizons from pathology to areas of psychological growth, the study of success-despite-the-odds gained momentum.

In this book, I examine what happens during these times. Why is it that some people who face adversity come out stronger for it? When we look at individuals who succeeded even though they were not "supposed" to, how do they go about living their lives differently? What can we learn from them? Are there core qualities that can boost us past our own self-imposed limits? How do we stay strong when everything around us tries to pull us down?

Succeeding When You're Supposed to Fail is an attempt to find answers to those questions.

1

Tunneling

Located along the banks of the Piscataquis River, just ninety miles south of the Canadian border, the sleepy town of Howland, Maine, has managed to keep much of its rural charm intact over the years. The most exciting news around town nowadays in Howland is a tourist spotting an occasional moose or bald eagle. But back in 1894 the town was ground zero of an intriguing mystery, one that defies our deepest assumptions about the resilience of the human spirit.

During the summer of that year, on a warm July day, Percy Spencer was born. There was nothing unusual or extraordinary about Percy's birth or about his family. His father, Jasper Spencer, worked in Howland's sawmill. His mother, Myrtle, following the tradition of the times, stayed at home taking care of the household. Percy's childhood was set to be quite normal, and so it was at first. But when he was just a toddler, tragedy struck at the sawmill. A rotating saw unexpectedly splintered, and the centripetal force sent shards flying in all directions. One of the pieces struck Percy's father, who died almost instantly.

The news sent Percy's mother into shock. The disaster proved too much for her to handle, and soon after the incident she fled the family home, never to return. Now orphaned, with no one to take care of him, young Percy was sent to live with his aunt and uncle.

Losing one's parents, especially at such a formative age, obviously has a lasting emotional impact. But fortunately for Percy, he had a roof over his head and family who loved him. He developed a special bond with his uncle, who became like a father to him. They both enjoyed tinkering with machinery. When Percy was just five, his uncle brought home a steam log hauler—essentially a locomotive that did not require train tracks—that was in need of repair. The large machine had recently broken down in the heavy winter snow, and Percy's uncle had been entrusted with its care. The mechanical wonder was like nothing Percy had ever seen before, and his excitement was palpable.

Percy also developed a love of nature and animals and spent much of his free time in the woods. On one occasion he spotted a cougar—one of the last remaining in Maine—up in a tree. But just as young Percy was acclimating to his new life, tragedy struck once more. When he was seven, his uncle died. The loss was a crushing blow to the family emotionally, but it also took a huge financial toll. Times were hard, and although Percy showed a penchant for learning, he was forced to drop out of school before completing the fifth grade to help support the family. The remainder of his childhood consisted of an adult regimen: wake up before dawn, put in a full day at the spool mill, and return home after sundown.

Put yourself, for a moment, in young Percy's shoes. You have no memories of your biological parents. Your mother left you when you were an infant. Your uncle, who was like a father to you, died when you were in second grade. And armed with only a fifth-grade education, you now spend every workday performing manual labor. It wouldn't be surprising if your sense of trust in the world around you began to erode. "Everyone who loves me either ends up dying or leaving," you might start to reason. You might even go as far as to blame yourself for the disasters that occurred: "Why is this happening to me? Why did my mother abandon me? Is my life always going to be filled with hardships?" Eventually, even a hardy soul can lose strength.

Difficult life events can take a psychological toll on an individual. Indeed, the notion that traumatic life events cause psychological harm seems so obvious that for many years psychologists assumed that it was virtually always the case. Experience a significant hardship, the belief went, and your life will be impacted for the worse.

This harm-leads-to-distress model of human psychology became a truism in the field—that is, until psychologist Emmy Werner came along. A newly minted Ph.D. with a specialty in developmental psychology, Werner had no idea she was about to throw her entire discipline into disarray. As a young professor, Werner spent most of her time performing statistical analyses on a project that tracked mothers and their babies living in Kauai, the westernmost island of the Hawaiian archipelago. When the project's chief researcher retired, Werner inherited the project's data. For a developmental psychologist, it was a gold mine. The first thing she did was to broaden the study's scope and follow a cohort of children from birth onward, tracking their performance over the course of their lives. Instead of observing participants in an artificial laboratory setting, she monitored real people living their lives.

To collect the new data, Werner assembled a team of professionals—social workers, nurses, physicians, a clinical psychologist—who helped her track the children. The researchers even collected prenatal data. Essentially, the study subjects, all 698 of them, were recruited as participants before they were even born.

"At the time, the focus of our study and others like it," Werner explained to me, "was very much on risk." Remember that psychologists were under the impression that children who grew up in difficult environments would inevitably develop psychological distress. Werner wanted to measure how these kids fared in the face of adversity.

Although some of the children that Werner followed were at risk, a large group that essentially served as a control came from healthy, normal backgrounds. For the most part, those children led completely ordinary, regular lives. In other words, they were not exposed to any major life stressors and enjoyed supportive home environments. And, as you might expect, for the most part they performed well in school, stayed out of serious trouble, and did not manifest any major psychological issues.

The other children from the cohort, though, were born into difficult circumstances. Like Percy Spencer, who struggled with financial and emotional loss in rural Maine, those children faced any number of obstacles. Most lived in poverty. Many of their parents suffered from alcoholism and mental illness, or were not around at all. Among this group of children, most, unfortunately, did not fare well. Their grades were poor. They acted out in school or got into trouble with the police. Many of these children eventually dropped out of school and became teenage parents. Unfortunately, that is what Werner expected to find.

But, surprisingly, that wasn't the case with *all* of the Kauai children who lived in deprived environments. Some of them managed to buck the trend. To Werner's—and eventually the wider psychological community's—surprise, about a third of the kids who came from disadvantaged backgrounds blossomed to lead rich and successful lives. They performed well in school. They formed healthy connections with their teachers and peers. As adults they were mentally strong and had successful careers. It's as if their tough upbringing had left virtually no mark on how they turned out.

It's worth pausing for a moment to consider what a radical shift Werner's findings presented from the psychological orthodoxy. Her study called into question the most basic tenet of psychological behaviorism: that there's a solid cause-and-effect relationship between the events in our past and our current psychological well-being. If the Kauai data were accurate, it meant that psychologists would have to redefine everything they thought they knew about basic human psychology.

At first, psychologists weren't sure what to make of Werner's results. Could it be that these miracle kids were just a fluke? Or perhaps there was something unique about the island or culture of Kauai that made it easier for disadvantaged kids to thrive? Even Werner was a bit dubious of the results. "I was wondering myself," she admitted when we talked, "whether there was a statistical problem." Maybe she had made a mistake analyzing the results, she thought.

But Werner's findings proved to be accurate. Two other pioneers in the field, Norman Garmezy and Michael Rutter, independently discovered this same "unlikely success" phenomenon. Other scientists further substantiated Werner's findings with their own research. In one major study, psychologists in Copenhagen investigated children who were raised by schizophrenic mothers. They found that although as a group they were more susceptible to developing psychological problems than average people, a significant portion of the kids led productive lives despite the chaotic conditions in which they grew up. Another longitudinal study found that among children who faced abject poverty, a subgroup of individuals emerged who transcended their difficult upbringing. All around the world—from England to Sweden to Australia—social scientists observed situations where individuals bucked the trend and rose out of their circumstances.

In one of the most comprehensive and telling studies to date, psychologists in New Zealand tracked a group of 1,265 children, all born in 1977, from birth to age twenty-one. The team followed the children closely and recorded every conceivable relevant piece of information they could find: their family's financial situation, their interactions at home, their conduct at school, their psychological functioning, any alcohol or drug use, and any signs of destructive tendencies. When they analyzed the body of data, the psychologists found that half of the children were leading normal lives with no significant hardships. Roughly 40 percent of them faced some obstacles—maybe their family life was a little shaky or they acted out in school. But about 10 percent of the children faced extreme hardships. They came from broken homes, lived in poverty, witnessed or experienced domestic violence, and had parents who struggled with substance abuse. But even growing up under these severe conditions, half of the children from this group fared well. They did not develop any alcohol or other drug dependence, displayed no psychological pathology, and did not get into trouble with the law. A third of them, the researchers found, did not exhibit any residual psychological symptoms, such as depression or anxiety.

But what about individuals who are exposed to the toughest and most unfortunate set of circumstances? The American psychologists Kerry Bolger and Charlotte Patterson identified a group of 107 elementary school children who were the victims of abuse and neglect. Bolger and Patterson tracked these children over a period of three years and found that most of them, understandably, showed at least some deficiencies or problem areas in their peer relations, academic achievement, general behavior, self-esteem, or psychological well-being. But even among this group of neglected and abused children, a few still managed to operate at or above grade level for at least a year on *all* of the key dimensions measured: they formed healthy relationships with other children, performed well in school, behaved well, developed a healthy self-esteem, and demonstrated no psychological problems over an extended period of time.

No matter how dire the circumstances, within every large group, psychologists now realize, a subset of individuals will emerge who manage to thrive despite everything they have endured. They overcome their life condition to prosper emotionally, psychologically, interpersonally, and in terms of their careers. It's as if these individuals are somehow adversity-proof; they seem to *tunnel* their way under or through harsh barriers to emerge virtually unscathed on the other side.

Consider two children who seem nearly identical. They live in the same neighborhood, attend the same schools, deal with similar family dynamics, and face the same issues of adversity. One child succumbs to the environmental and emotional turmoil around him and stumbles into a life filled with challenges and difficulties. The other child, faced with the same hardships, somehow manages to tunnel his way through the adversity he faces and goes on to lead a healthy, successful life. What causes two similar individuals to take such divergent paths?

When it comes to physical health, we know the factors responsible for a positive outcome. Eat nutritious food, but don't eat too much; be physically active; have regular access to medical care; and you're on your way to a healthy life. Similarly, when it comes to education, we know that studying hard, receiving support and encouragement at home, and having good teachers make a huge difference. But when it comes to overcoming adversity for children and adults, whether they are facing small challenges or severe ones—most of us are in the dark.

Why do some people manage to overcome or tunnel through obstacles that defeat most others? Why is it that individuals who seem destined for failure become successful? What are the psychological factors that allow someone to defeat the odds?

The concept of tunneling in scientific discourse originates, oddly enough, in the field of quantum physics. It's used to describe the counterintuitive behavior of subatomic particles. Decades before psychologists began investigating unlikely success, physicists were grappling with some unlikely mysteries of their own.

In the 1920s physicists realized that the universe seemed to be breaking its own rules, and no one quite knew why. It all started with two perplexing puzzles concerning the very large and the very small. The first mystery involves the sun. According to classical principles of physics, the sun is not supposed to shine. In order for a star to be able to produce enough heat to glow, hydrogen atoms need to fuse to produce helium. But hydrogen atoms naturally *repel* each other because of their similar electric charge. In order for hydrogen atoms to fuse, they need to be heated to an extremely high temperature—ten billion degrees, to be exact—so that they can travel fast enough to overcome their inherent repulsion. And this is where the big problem came up. Astrophysicists determined that although the sun is hot, it's not *ten billion degrees* hot. Even at its core, the sun's temperature reaches only one-tenth of 1 percent of the heat necessary for fusion to occur. So how does the sun manage to shine?

The other mystery that preoccupied physicists involves radioactive decay. In simple terms, a radioactive element decays when it loses energy by emitting ionizing particles from its nucleus. But just as hydrogen particles are not supposed to be able to fuse together inside the sun, radioactive elements, according to the principles of classical physics, are not supposed to decay. That's because the force holding a nucleus together is so strong that particles should never be able to suddenly escape. It would be as if you were to jump up and down and in one of those attempts you suddenly managed to break free of Earth's gravity and found yourself floating off into space. The nuclear force inside an element should be far too strong to allow particles to escape the nucleus. But physicists have repeatedly found that particles can and do leave the nucleus, seemingly without regard for the basic laws of physics.

So how did physicists account for these two impossibilities? It turns out that subatomic particles are subject to two differing and often clashing sets of laws—classical "commonsense" laws and tunneling "probability cloud" laws. The classical laws are clear-cut: there are limits on what physical objects can do, based on the classical laws of physics. The tunneling laws, on the other hand, are much murkier. Every subatomic particle has a "probability cloud" that determines its location. The probability cloud contains all imaginable possibilities, even those that defy classical rules. The process of determining what actually happens and which possibility is actualized is completely random, and no one fully understands it. Physicists have become very good at determining the precise odds involved in this relocation process, so that they can predict with great accuracy the odds for where a particle could appear, but no one understands how the probability cloud works or why it exists. Microscopic particles routinely appear and disappear as if they're using some invisible *Star Trek* transporter.

The important thing to note for our purposes is that tunneling supersedes the classical laws of physics. When the random tunneling probability situates a particle in a place it's not "supposed" to be able to get to, it becomes situated there. That's how subatomic particles are able to overcome the impossible. If the probability cloud positions a particle outside a uranium nucleus, the nucleus decays. And if a hydrogen atom is randomly positioned very near another hydrogen atom, they fuse to produce helium.

Even large objects like human beings are subject to the effects of a probability cloud. But the more massive an object, the tinier the probability cloud. That's why you don't see chairs and tables and people disappearing and reappearing all over the place. Still, physicists calculate that if you press your hand against a wall and repeat the action for about a dozen billion years, on one of those trillions of attempts your hand will succeed in tunneling through the wall to emerge on the other side, leaving both the wall and your hand intact.

The point about quantum tunneling is that subatomic particles routinely defy classical or traditional laws, achieving what on the surface would seem impossible. Similarly, in the psychological world, certain individuals are able to defy classical psychological barriers and achieve improbable success. This gets at something fundamental about human nature.

Whereas in quantum mechanics the movement and location of subatomic particles are random—no one can determine whether one particle will tunnel in favor of another or even when such tunneling will take place—psychological tunneling can be deconstructed and traced back to its originating factors. And fortunately, unlike with the quantum probability cloud, the odds or probability of overcoming our psychological limits can be actively increased as we shift our attitudes about life, the world around us, and our capabilities. Scientists in developmental psychology, organizational behavior, management, and clinical psychology have begun to decipher the hidden qualities that define people who are able to tunnel through life barriers. What emerges are the underlying psychological factors and characteristics that give tunnelers their power.

Most of us are guided the majority of the time by well-understood psychological laws or principles. We become motivated when we receive praise and experience success, and we feel deflated and uninspired when we run into significant obstacles. But that doesn't have to be the case. We can learn how to flourish despite the seemingly impenetrable barriers that we've learned to accept as reality. Think of all the times in our lives when we stop ourselves short—when we do not ask out the person we have a crush on in high school or shy away from a challenging project at work or give up on an exercise regimen we know would be good for us—just because when faced with stumbling blocks and obstructions, we give up because they seem too overwhelming.

This book explores why some people, faced with deficiencies and limitations, are able to tunnel through the barriers before them. How does such tunneling come about? How can we actively put these tunneling maneuvers to work in our personal and professional lives?

Working as a psychologist, I have had the privilege of interacting with a number of clients who are tunnelers. When they relate the difficulties in their lives, which are often filled with unimaginable hardships, I'm constantly intrigued by their ability to fight through their difficulties and surmount the challenges that would keep most people back. What allows them to go on to lead extremely successful lives—to graduate from college, form loving relationships, and lead successful careers? When I bring this to their attention and ask them how or why they think it is that they were able to overcome their disadvantages, they are puzzled. They don't realize that they are tunneling or doing anything out of the ordinary. Then I lay out the case before them: look at everything that you've gone through, at what you have endured, yet somehow you've managed to escape the poverty of your childhood, the dysfunction of your family, or the fact that you grew up with an alcoholic father or without a father at all. What do you think made the difference for you? I ask. But they nearly always have the same answer: "I don't know. I never thought about it this way before. I'm not sure I can put my finger on it." But as we spend more time together, it becomes increasingly evident that they lead their lives differently from most of us.

Throughout the course of this book we'll meet tunnelers of all ages—from POWs to CEOs, in places from the classroom to the boardroom—and uncover the underlying qualities that help them defy the odds. With the growing interest in positive psychology, there's recently been an upsurge in the number of research studies devoted to the investigation of the "unlikely success" phenomenon. They have uncovered the essential qualities that differentiate tunnelers from most people: How do tunnelers interact differently with the world around them? How do they perceive and make sense of life events? Do they have different attitudes and beliefs?

We already met our first tunneler earlier in the chapter. In rural Maine, without any financial means to continue his schooling, young Percy Spencer had no choice but to become a day laborer. With so much stacked against him—his father and uncle's deaths, abandonment by his mother, financial difficulties, and a lack of formal education—Spencer might have been expected to live out his life as an undistinguished laborer, with no real prospects for improvement. But as his grandson Rod Spencer explained to me, "Gramps operated on a different track."

The fact that he couldn't attend school didn't stop Spencer from gaining an education. He taught himself everything he could about math, science, and technology. In his free time he conjured up mental challenges—an algebra problem, an engineering quandary—and spent hours solving them. He was determined to continue his education through an alternative route. He called the process "solving my own situation."

Spencer didn't follow the course that fate seemed to have laid out for him. Instead of succumbing to circumstances, he somehow tunneled to a future full of possibilities, refusing to accept that any doors to advancement were permanently closed to him. When Spencer was sixteen, the local paper mill wanted to modernize and go electric. But back then, no one knew much about electricity. Spencer didn't either, but, having had a lifelong passion for all things mechanical, he was interested in the project. He had come to a tunneling fork in the road. From a classical psychology perspective, most people in Spencer's situation would have reasoned that they knew nothing about electricity and had no business getting involved in something that was clearly over their head. Remember, Spencer hadn't even finished elementary school. He was a teenage boy with no particular skill set.

But Spencer reframed the challenge as a unique opportunity and threw himself at it. Without receiving any on-the-job training, he learned everything he needed by working side by side with two other electricity enthusiasts. By the time the project was completed, Spencer was a full-fledged electrician. And he kept making those types of tunneling choices throughout his life. Inspired by the wireless telegraph operators who played a crucial role in the rescue of *Titanic* survivors, Spencer decided to join the navy in the hope of being sent to radio school, despite his limited education. "I just got hold of a lot of textbooks and taught myself while I was standing watch at night," he explained.

By the time Spencer was fifty, he was working as a senior vice president at a defense contractor company he had helped co-found. His love of animals from his childhood days in the Maine woods remained a passion into adulthood. Because he spent most of his working hours indoors, he carried a peanut bar with him, his grandson explained to me, so that he could feed the squirrels and birds whenever he got the chance. One day, during a visit to one of the company's labs, he experienced a peculiar sensation. He could've sworn that the peanut bar inside his pocket was melting.

He quickly reached for the candy and sure enough, the peanut bar *was* turning liquid. Further investigation identified the culprit as a magnetron, a high-powered vacuum tube that generates electromagnetic waves. The lab manufactured the magnetrons for use in radars, so nobody gave a second thought about the machine's power to melt food. Intrigued, Spencer sent someone to fetch popcorn kernels. When Spencer placed the kernels close to the magnetron, they began to pop.

Spencer wasn't the first person to realize that magnetrons have the power to heat food, but he was the first one to follow his curiosity through and investigate. Instead of sticking to what he knew, he decided to seize on the challenge and explore the possibilities. He slightly modified the magnetron and invented the "radar range," or what we more commonly know today as the microwave oven. Every time you heat up your lunch or warm up your leftovers, you're relying on a machine that was developed thanks to the ingenuity of a tunneler.

Percy Spencer's journey is unique, but most of us can identify tunnelers in our lives. Maybe it's a relative with an amazing life story or a friend who overcame harrowing circumstances. It might even be someone you never met but whose journey has inspired you. Think of Barack Obama's unlikely life path to the presidency; Sonia Sotomayor's rise to Supreme Court Justice; or Scott Brown's ascent to the U.S. Senate after early-childhood poverty and abuse. Look for tunnelers, and you'll spot them in the most unlikely places.

Take the high-fashion industry. We associate it with images

of glamour and elegance, especially when it comes to designers whose clientele includes Beyoncé, Elizabeth Hurley, and Angelina Jolie. But as the noted fashion designer Elie Tahari will tell you, his life didn't start out with any of the charm or allure linked with the industry. Born to Iranian immigrants in Jerusalem in 1952, Tahari never got to know his family well. His parents divorced when he was just a small child. Shortly afterward, his father abandoned the family. When Tahari's mother couldn't provide basic care for her children, social services had to intervene, and Tahari spent the rest of his childhood living in various orphanages.

When he was in his early twenties, Tahari decided to visit New York on a whim. But because he had so little money saved, he could afford to budget only three dollars per day for all of his expenses. In Manhattan, even back in the early 1970s, three dollars didn't take you very far, and the young traveler was forced to spend most nights sleeping on Central Park benches. But instead of feeling miserable, Tahari viewed his experience as an adventure. "I didn't think I didn't have a place to sleep," he remembers. "I thought I was camping. I was camping in New York."

Eventually, Tahari managed to land a job changing light-bulbs on the street. In the evenings he supplemented his income by working in a clothing boutique, mainly so that he could meet women. Tahari had no initial interest in clothes or design, but as he got to know his customers, he discovered he had a knack for predicting what they'd like. He tried his hand at coming up with a few of his own designs and eventually created his own line. His biggest problem, though, was that nobody knew about him.

If you're a recent immigrant with limited funds, with no connections in the industry, and your only asset is your creative talent, your options are limited. Tahari knew he had to rely on himself. When he heard about a fashion show that was going to be held at a local hotel, he secretly made his way to the topmost floor, carrying as many of his clothing articles with him as he could. He then hung his designs on the hallway walls, hoping to attract some attention. His flea market–style tactics might seem crude, but they attracted a crowd that grew larger and larger. Tahari achieved his goal; if anything, he garnered too much attention. When the hotel security noticed all the hoopla going on on the topmost floor, they came to investigate.

Without missing a beat, Tahari quickly repacked his designs and set up shop on the floor below. He kept an eye out for security, and whenever he sensed they were heading his way, he'd relocate to a lower floor. By day's end, Tahari had made his way through all of the hotel's floors, collecting orders for 250,000 articles of clothing—wildly surpassing his initial targets. "I had to succeed," Tahari explains matter-of-factly years later. "Failure meant I would have to be homeless again." The event marked the start of what would become a fashion empire currently valued at half a billion dollars.

Far away from the glittering lights of New York, in a small north Florida town mired in crime, another tunneler, Marshawn "Mardy" Gilyard, was trying to overcome his own share of obstacles. Born in 1986, Gilyard was raised by a single mother who worked long hours. To make matters worse, money was tight, the electricity at home often got disconnected, and access to food was limited. As young children, Gilyard and his brother often had to prepare their own meals themselves. They whipped up less-than-spectacular culinary creations with the limited ingredients available to them. A favorite was a mayonnaise sandwich—prepared literally, with just bread and mayonnaise. Another of Gilyard's faux entrées consisted of a bowl of cereal with water. Gilyard made the best of a bad situation. "Just close your eyes and chew it real slow," he explains, "and it'll taste like a porterhouse."

Gilyard didn't let the situation at home get the best of him. He focused on his passion, playing football. A fast runner with exceptional hand-to-eye coordination, Gilyard grew to become a star wide receiver for his high school team. In 2005 his years of dedication paid off: he landed a scholarship to play for the University of Cincinnati. Once he was in Cincinnati, though, the academic demands coupled with the rigorous football schedule proved too much for the young athlete. When his grades suffered, his coach kicked Gilyard off the team, automatically revoking his scholarship.

Imagine being a teenager, hundreds of miles away from home, and learning that your dream of playing college football has been shattered. On top of that, you no longer have the financial support to continue your studies.

Devastated, Gilyard called home and broke the news to his mom. He'd be back home soon, he let her know. But Gilyard's mother would have none of it. She didn't want to see her son quit and told him to stay put in Cincinnati. Find a way to make it work, she insisted. "And if we see you here," she admonished, "we'll ship you back."

But sticking it out in Cincinnati was going to be tough. With the football scholarship gone, Gilyard now owed the university $10,000 for his out-of-state tuition. Given his financial situation, the debt felt like $10 million. But Gilyard had another talent besides football, one that he had cultivated as a young child: the ability to make do with limited resources. Just as he had taught himself to conjure up perceived delicacies from scraps of food in his boyhood kitchen, he now had to find a creative way to generate money with limited resources. To minimize expenses, he moved out of his dorm and lived out of his car, crashing at friends' homes for the night. He juggled four jobs—as a cook in an Italian restaurant, a package deliverer, a kitchen knife salesman, and a construction worker. And, amazingly, on top of everything, while braving the Cincinnati winter, Gilyard made time to volunteer, working with kids and feeding the homeless.

In the spring of 2007 Gilyard's effort paid off. Cincinnati got a new coach, who reviewed Gilyard's tapes and decided to give the player a second chance—if he promised to work harder in school and pay the debt he owed the university. Gilyard was ecstatic. He had already saved some money, and soon he was able to save more and rejoin the team. In 2009, as a senior wide receiver, he helped lead Cincinnati to an undefeated regular season. Before heading out onto the field for his last game as a collegiate athlete, he paused to take in the moment. He reflected on his struggles and everything he had endured. And before he knew it, tears started streaming down his face. "I relish every millisecond I have here," he told the supportive crowd of teammates and reporters who gathered around him. "I don't expect nothing. Sometimes you might feel like people owe you something. I don't."

ESPN's Pat Forde was one of the reporters in that locker room. "I don't think I've ever seen a player cry at a pregame news conference," he remembered as he tried to capture the intensity of the experience. "He went on talking, not even bothering to wipe the tears away." The story became the inspirational high-light of the 2009 football season, and a few months later Gilyard signed a four-year, $2.3 million deal to play wide receiver for the St. Louis Rams.

Tunnelers, with their tenacity and can-do attitude, bring a unique perspective to any business or group. It's a quality that Richard Shaw, Stanford's dean of admission and financial aid, actively seeks out when determining admissions. At a university that receives more than 25,000 applications annually and turns away more than 90 percent of them, the admission officers can afford to be picky. "What's beautiful about Stanford," explains Dean Shaw, "is that to a great extent it is color-blind. Stanford is a global university. We're going to try and get the best kids. We don't set quotas or time frames." In other words, Stanford has a lot of flexibility in selecting its students. Deciding which students to accept is a tough decision, though. "To be honest with you," he explains, "when you look at Stanford applicants, the vast major-ity—eighty percent or so—are eligible. They're strong." That is, they have what it takes to make it. So Stanford has to look beyond the basic numbers.

During a homecoming talk that Shaw gave to Stanford

alumni, he shed light on one of the hidden qualities he's looking for. He explained that he finds a student with a 3.5 GPA from a school located on the wrong side of the tracks more fascinating than one with a 4.0 GPA from an elite school. In a less-well-to-do school, you find many more young people who, as Shaw puts it, "have no control over the cards they were dealt." Pulling off a 3.5 GPA means that they had to tunnel through a lot of obstacles to achieve academic excellence, often without the benefit of the best teachers, highly educated parents, or special tutoring. "So they might be in inner-city high schools," Shaw said, "and if they're the best in those high schools, then they have a shot at coming to Stanford."

It's not just about diversity, Shaw elaborated. When you have a senior who lives in the suburbs and receives a 4.0 GPA, you know that this student has probably learned to "play the system." Shaw didn't mean it in a derogatory sense, but those high school students have learned what they need to do in order to excel within the system. You know you're getting a bright, capable student. But with the 3.5 GPA student from a poor inner-city school system, in addition to getting a bright, capable student, you're getting someone who is extremely motivated who knows how to deal with and overcome adversity. Those applicants had to fight their way into doing well in school. They know what it's like to face down constant challenges at home, in their neighborhoods, at school. They bring a quality of perseverance and resilience to their schoolwork and to life. And they will bring that to their careers later, as well. It's not that Shaw—or any dean of undergraduate admissions—doesn't appreciate students who work hard and come from well-to-do backgrounds, accomplished families, and strong school systems. It's just that in putting together a freshman class at Stanford, he recognizes the kind of inner strength a student has to have to achieve a 3.5 GPA in a tough environment. In other words, a tunneler. That kind of quality is enough to pique anyone's interest.

In our investigation into tunneling, we'll explore the qualities behind unlikely success. They fall into three major categories, marking the three sections of this book. In the first section we're going to look at the *inner drive* that allows tunnelers to break away from the path in which their life seems to be taking them. Tunnelers hold themselves accountable in a way that is different from most of us. But tunnelers also tend to have a unique ability to derive meaning from their circumstances when none seems to exist. And they exhibit a relentlessness in pursuing their goals.

In the second section we'll investigate tunnelers' *orientation*. We usually think of people who overcome adversity as being tough—people who have a type A personality. And tunnelers are indeed tough, but not in the way we might think. They have a remarkable ability to approach life with an even-tempered disposition. They don't get bogged down and stressed out by life events. They find creative ways to use humor to increase their stamina and forge social ties.

It's easy to think of tunnelers as strong individuals who don't need the help of others to be happy or successful. In fact, as we'll see in the final section, the opposite is true—tunnelers, it turns out, *rely heavily* on the help and support of others. They have at least one person in their lives whom they trust implicitly and on whom they can count, someone who cares for them unconditionally.

There are two important things to realize about tunnelers. The first is that they are not that different from the rest of us. They're not superhuman. It's just that on the continuum of personality traits, their resilience, persistence, and ability to find ways to overcome adversity are more pronounced. They're at the more extreme end of the spectrum. There is nothing to prevent any of us from developing a similar mind-set, or making a similar shift.

The other important thing about tunnelers is the universality of the qualities that make them outstanding. The same qualities that enable tunnelers to succeed in one context or set of circumstances work equally well when facing a completely different set of challenges. Tunnelers, whether young or old, starting out their careers or on top of their field, rely on the same principles to help them advance.

Our investigation into the nature of tunnelers starts with an accidental discovery made by a psychologist who has grown strangely ambivalent about his contribution.

DRIVE

2

The Limelight Effect

It was an awkward scene. Standing behind the podium was the psychologist Julian Rotter, one of the most prolific researchers in the field of social learning theory. Born in Brooklyn in 1916 to Jewish immigrants, Rotter rose to become the chairman of the Society for Personality and Social Psychology of the American Psychological Association (APA). Toward the end of his career, the APA bestowed upon him its most prestigious honor: the Distinguished Scientific Contribution Award. Rotter was about to join an exclusive Who's Who of American psychologists—a list that includes the likes of B. F. Skinner, Carl Rogers, Albert Bandura, and Noam Chomsky.

But as he was delivering his acceptance speech at the award ceremony, the audience couldn't help but notice that instead of basking in the moment, Rotter seemed preoccupied. At times he sounded annoyed, even angry. At one point he went as far as to accuse "many psychologists" of being "inadequately trained in theory." His audience hadn't expected to hear such strong words on such a celebratory occasion. Why the harsh tone? As far as Rotter was concerned, he was up on stage for all the wrong reasons, honored for a contribution he thought had been blown way out of proportion. What Rotter was trying to communicate to his puzzled audience was that the psychological community had gotten him all wrong.

It all began, innocently enough, with an obscure observation that Rotter himself had almost overlooked. Much of Rotter's career was spent conducting experiments on social learning. He found that when people perform well on a task and receive praise for a job well done, they develop a positive self-image about their abilities. The opposite happens when they perform poorly. Nothing surprising about that.

But there was an important exception. Over time, Rotter noticed that some of his subjects failed to adjust their self-assessment when asked to evaluate their performance. No matter how strongly or poorly they performed on previous tasks or what messages they received from others, they failed to recognize themselves as agents of change. In other words, they took no personal credit for their behavior.

At first Rotter didn't make much of this anomaly, dismissing it as a curious oddity. But things came into focus during a routine clinical supervision meeting Rotter had with one of his doctoral students. The supervision session, which started out much like any other, would end up altering Rotter's professional career. On that fateful day Rotter's clinical trainee appeared dejected. The student had been working for weeks with an unusually difficult client who complained of interpersonal difficulties. At the beginning of treatment, the clinical progression had appeared promising. When the doctoral student had suggested to his client that he should change some of his maladaptive behaviors, the client had readily agreed. And sure enough, after a few weeks, the patient's problems had begun to abate. So far, so good. But, oddly enough, the client wasn't happy with the results.

Instead of taking pride in his accomplishments or thanking the therapist-in-training for his help, the client, as Rotter tells it, "persistently explained away the successes as a matter of luck and not likely to happen again." The doctoral student was stuck. No matter how hard he tried, he couldn't convince his client that his life circumstances had improved as a result of the work he had been doing and all of the effort he had put in. In essence, the patient failed to link his actions with the resulting outcome. "[The client] appeared, in most situations," Rotter later explained, "to feel that what happened to him was entirely beyond his control."

What do you do with someone who stubbornly dismisses progress as a fluke or random event? In thinking about this puzzling case, Rotter had an astounding insight. This client, Rotter surmised, had much in common with the laboratory participants who failed to adjust their own self-expectations despite their improved performance and the feedback they received. In both cases individuals categorically failed to link their actions with changes in their lives. If you believe you don't really have any substantial control over your life, why should your expectations shift?

Rotter published an article about his observation, and it took the psychological community by storm. The phenomenon eventually came to be known in academic circles as "locus of control," but a more descriptive term is the *limelight effect*. Picture a dark theater with a singular beam of light pointed at a single actor on stage. If you were in that theater, you would naturally focus on that actor. Wherever the limelight would travel to next would become your new center of attention. Similarly in life, we have a psychological limelight that focuses our attention. What's most interesting is the direction of our limelight. Is our limelight pointed at ourselves or is it directed at the world around us? In other words, do we view ourselves as the protagonist in our lives or do we pay more attention to people and events around us?

People with an externally directed limelight—like the laboratory participants and the psychotherapy client—interpret events in their lives through elements outside themselves: luck, fate, other people's actions, random incidents, the ways the world operates, or society's rules. Because their limelight is pointed away from them, "externals" don't consider their own actions to be an important contributor to what's going on in their lives. That is, they see themselves as secondary participants, in the background, without having much control over what happens to them.

At the other extreme are people with an internally directed limelight. They take full responsibility for the events that unfold in their lives, viewing themselves as central participants.

This simple difference in the direction of our limelight—whether or not we have an internal or external perspective—plays a key role in determining our ability to overcome adversity and achieve success. But what does it really mean to view things from an internal or external perspective? Try this limelight direction exercise. Think back over your professional (or school) career, touching on all the important events that have taken place: the opportunities that came your way that you either seized or let pass by, the highs and lows, the serendipitous events, the pleasant surprises and jarring shocks. What made things turn out the way they did? How much of your career—or, for that matter, your personal life, friendships, and family and love life—can you personally account for? How much of it is your own doing, and how much dropped into your lap?

It turns out that how you answer these questions reveals important information about your personality and even the future trajectory of your life. To see how, we'll delve a little deeper into the two different limelight personality types. Externals, remember, shine the light on events outside of their immediate control. If they had to reflect on their career, they'd likely point a finger at events that had little to do with their actions or behavior. They might talk about their supervisors and the decisions they made, the state of the economy, the way in which office politics, family demands, and other unexpected events conspired to bring them to where they are today. If any of these dynamics had shifted even in minor ways, they feel, their entire career path could've turned out very differently. They believe that in life, as in the formation of a weather system, many different elements come together; chance plays a major role. Just as it would be ridiculous to expect that you can influence the weather by flapping your arms to create wind, the argument goes, it's futile to believe that you play a major role in determining your career track. According to externals, the only thing that's certain is that believing that you have significant control over life's complex events is nonsense.

Internals, on the other hand, answer the same set of questions very differently. They point the limelight at themselves and focus on specific choices they made that influenced their career outcome: attending a good college, deciding to take on a challenging project, maintaining a good attitude at work, seeking out new opportunities, pursuing further education, being prompt and efficient, mastering new skills, networking with the right people, being dependable and reliable. Of course, they would also recall the mistakes they had made that had held them back: not obtaining as much training as they could have, not putting in enough effort, getting caught up in counterproductive office politics.

Most of us shift our limelight back and forth: we take credit for some things (especially the positive), but we also externalize responsibility to forces or events outside our control (especially the negative). From time to time, though, we come across people who represent the extremes of limelight direction styles. The character George Costanza, of *Seinfeld*, serves as a perfect illustration. What makes George so uniquely comical is not just his laziness or his miserly behavior but the extraordinary lengths he goes to in order to keep his limelight focused on events and people outside of himself.

Take the time George began to second-guess his engagement to his fiancée. He took himself completely out of the equation by blaming his friend Jerry for bailing out on their plan to get serious and find a spouse. "What happened to the pact?" George laments. "We were both gonna change. We shook hands on a pact. Did you not shake my hand on it, huh?" In George's mind, the "pact"—or, more precisely, Jerry's lack of follow-through—is the root cause of George's misery: If it hadn't been for the pact, he would've never pursued his current relationship. If it hadn't been for the pact, he wouldn't be stuck now with a fiancée he didn't truly want to marry. Never mind that no one put a gun to George's head or that he never took responsibility for his role in the "pact" or that he failed to seriously consider the options he had to extricate himself from the situation.

George points his limelight outwardly almost as a reflex action, without even thinking about it. When he accidentally damages Jerry's car during another incident, he once again shifts responsibility to someone besides himself—this time to Elaine. "You had to move the [car] mirror?" he complains. "You threw off my equilibrium." Whatever that means.

When there's no one specific to hold accountable, George blames his parents. "I come from a long line of quitters," he laments, only half jokingly. "My father was a quitter, my grandfather was a quitter. I was raised to fail." Even when George finds fault with himself, the *cause* of his misery always originates from without.

Now contrast George Costanza to someone completely opposite: Abraham Lincoln. The comparison itself is outlandish. They are so completely different from each other in almost every way. While George consistently attributes events in his life to the shortcomings of others, Lincoln held himself accountable for his upbringing and actions from a very young age. Growing up with little money and limited access to education, he looked to himself for solutions. As a child, he developed an interest in reading, but his family owned almost no books. Instead of accepting his fate or blaming his family's situation on bad luck, Lincoln looked to himself to remedy the situation. He walked long distances to borrow books from neighbors. As a teenager, he became interested in law. Once again his family didn't have the resources to help him. Instead of accepting his lot in life, he regularly made the trek to the nearest courthouse—a seventeen-mile walk—to watch attorneys in action. As president, he inherited a bankrupt country on the verge of a civil war. Instead of blaming his predecessor, he focused his attention on the things he could do, telling Congress that "we . . . hold the power and bear the responsibility."

What's so extraordinary about the differences between externals and internals is that it's not a question of who's right and who's wrong. Just as an optimist and a pessimist can look at the same exact situation and arrive at two completely different conclusions, an internal and an external can consider an identical life situation and come up with two completely different explanations of how it came to be. But as we'll soon see, when it comes to overcoming adversity, what's important is not the objective facts of the situation, it's how we position our psychological limelight that makes a difference. In other words, our perception of how reality came to be is more important than the reality itself.

That may seem like a radical statement. After all, we tend to think of our lives in terms of all the things that have happened to us, all the events that have shaped who we are. But it is the *process* of interpreting those events and piecing together our personal narrative, or life story, that makes such a difference. When it comes to overcoming adversity, longitudinal studies have found that a key quality separating tunnelers—individuals who have beaten the odds to achieve success—from those who succumb to adversity has to do with locus of control. Tunnelers focus on themselves as agents of change, adopting an internally directed limelight. To test how much of a difference our focus can have on our lives, a team of British researchers asked more than ten thousand ten-year-olds to take several cognitive and personality tests, including a locus-of-control survey. Twenty years later, when the study participants turned thirty, the researchers asked the subjects questions about their psychological health. Were they feeling distressed? Anxious? Depressed?

Now think back to when you were ten. You were certainly a very different person in so many ways. What did you think about the opposite sex? What was your favorite TV show? Favorite food? What were your interests? What did you want to do when you grew up? Despite all these differences, though, there are some aspects of your character that stand the test of time and deeply identify who you are. Surprisingly, the direction of your limelight is one of them. The researchers found that participants' orientation scores from *twenty years earlier* predicted their psychological well-being when they were thirty.

Those participants who attributed responsibility to themselves when they were ten were significantly less likely to experience psychological issues as adults. It's an astounding notion to consider. And it doesn't just stop with psychological well-being.

These child internals also had a reduced propensity to become overweight and were more likely to report being in overall good physical health at age thirty. Even when the researchers controlled for other possible explanations for overall health—such as education, social class, and intelligence—locus of control remained influential.

There are certain habits that we try to foster and encourage in children from a young age: eating healthfully, staying in school, not smoking, exercising regularly. We know that these behaviors have far-reaching consequences. Nevertheless, we usually don't think of psychological habits or ways of looking at the world as having just as long-lasting an effect on our mental and physical health. The various agencies and health care groups that wisely encourage us to eat healthfully and work out frequently would also do well to tout the benefits of adopting an internally focused limelight. Imagine, for instance, a revised food pyramid where limelight direction is one of the key ingredients. The academic literature is filled with study after study that links an internal attribution style that sees us as captains of our fate to positive qualities: higher grades in school, greater intelligence, even a longer life span. It's just that we're not used to thinking of our psychological habits as being as important to our health as our physical ones.

Why is it that an internal attribution of responsibility carries so many benefits and makes us more prone to succeed? A clever study conducted by a pair of psychiatrists from the University of Illinois College of Medicine at Peoria gives us a clue. The researchers placed an advertisement seeking married individuals who'd feel comfortable talking about their "marriage and their

thoughts, feelings, and behavior." When the couples came in to
the lab, they completed a thirty-two-item questionnaire that as-
sessed their marital satisfaction. Each participant also completed
a locus-of-control inventory. Finally each subject took a "provoc-
ative marital behaviors" test, an assessment tool that essentially
measures how often your spouse gets on your nerves.

When the researchers tabulated the results, they noticed a
curious pattern. As you might expect, participants who rated their
spouse high on the annoying incident inventory scored low on
overall marital satisfaction. After all, anger-arousing situations
take their toll on a marriage. But what was especially revealing
about the results was the effect that attribution of responsibility had on the men. Those men who rated their wives as being
pleasant and agreeable described their relationships as positive regardless of their individual limelight orientation. And this makes
sense. If you're happy with your spouse, you're likely to be happy
with your relationship regardless of how you attribute responsibility. But what about the men who described their wives as being
less pleasant? For those with an external focus, their frustration
with their relationship increased in direct proportion to their dis-
pleasure with their wife. The more they were annoyed with their
spouse, the higher their frustration level. But the men with an
internal locus of control maintained a low frustration level in their
relationship no matter how annoying they found their wife to be.

In other words, internals are not as easily affected by their
wives' actions as externals are. They're less likely to place the limelight on their wives in determining their satisfaction with the relationship. Externals, on the other hand, are much more volatile in

their reactions. When they find their wives to be extremely pleasant, their marital satisfaction score is sky-high. But their satisfaction level drops precipitously as their annoyance increases. Think of George Costanza on *Seinfeld*. Every time his fiancée, Susan, did or said anything that annoyed him, his relationship satisfaction plummeted. His well-being was largely dependent on her.

There's an important lesson here about the way in which attribution directional style affects our ability to deal with adversity. Externals experience greater ups and downs in their level of satisfaction. Their psychological ecosystem is more vulnerable because they interpret their reality based on what is going on around them at any given moment in time. Because they don't perceive themselves as having much power to implement change, their anxiety rises when they're in a difficult situation. They feel helpless, buffeted by forces beyond their control. When those with an internal locus of control experience adversity, they are less likely to succumb to the stressful situation. Instead of feeling overwhelmed by life or thinking to themselves, "This is not fair. What have I done to deserve this?" they reason, "What is it that I can do differently to create a better result? What changes can I make?"

An internally directed limelight is one of the key elements that drive psychological tunneling. When facing adversity and challenges, attributing responsibility to ourselves allows us to reclaim control of our lives and set a new course of action to respond to the events that are happening to us. Back in the nineteenth century, Elizabeth Cady Stanton, a pioneer of equality for women, seemed to have instinctively recognized this quality. Stanton dedicated her life to reforming laws that prohibited women from owning property, getting a divorce, and voting. She fought vehemently against socially conservative movements that sought to restrict women's rights and keep women sheltered from life's challenges. Though laws and social and religious mores kept women oppressed, she felt that no woman should have to accept her fate. When she was in her seventies, she addressed Congress, delivering a moving and eloquent address about the importance of having the freedom to be the captain of your ship. "Nothing strengthens the judgment and quickens the conscience like individual responsibility," she advised. "Nothing adds such dignity to character as the recognition of one's self-sovereignty."

More than a hundred years after Stanton spoke before Congress, a pair of business school professors from the University of Iowa put her tenets about personal responsibility to the test. They wanted to see how one's locus of control compared with other major psychological variables in predicting success in the workplace. They conducted a meta-analytical study, pooling information from relevant past research experiments. When they compared all the data across the studies, they found, as we might expect, that qualities such as emotional stability and being comfortable with one's skill set contribute to success. Interestingly, the studies revealed that an internal limelight orientation is just as important to both job satisfaction and job performance. In fact, they found that an internal locus of control is as powerful as self-esteem when it comes to on-the-job excellence. Think of all the ways in which we consciously build up a child's or an employee's self-confidence and self-esteem. How often do we emphasize the direction in which we point our psychological limelight?

Other research has found that individuals with an internal locus of control are much more likely to pursue entrepreneurial endeavors than are those with an external locus of control. During tough times, internals look at themselves to come up with a solution, rather than casting blame on a tough market or a bad economy. Successful entrepreneurs tend to ask themselves, "What is it that I can do to overcome this challenge?"

Still, even when we're aware of the benefits that come with an internally directed limelight, it can be difficult to retain this mind-set. Here's a case in point. Imagine that you need to catch a domestic flight leaving at 9:00 A.M. The night before you set your alarm clock for 6:30 A.M., figuring that'll give you an hour to get ready, thirty minutes to drive to the airport, and an hour to check in. Unfortunately, things don't pan out the way you expected.

Because of an overnight power outage, your electric alarm clock fails to function, and you oversleep. You wake up at 7:20 A.M. in a panic—and jump out of bed. You rush to get everything together and leave by 7:45. As you enter the freeway, traffic is unexpectedly slow. It turns out there's a small accident up ahead on the other side of the freeway. But traffic is stop-and-go even going in your direction. You keep checking the time as you slowly advance.

At 8:25 you finally arrive at the airport parking lot. Sprinting, you make it to the airline counter at 8:30, out of breath, ready to print your boarding pass. But the kiosks that print the boarding passes are all down. You flag an airline employee, who helps you troubleshoot the problem. By the time you're set to go and head toward the security check-in line, it's 8:43. You realize that you're going to be cutting it really close.

At this point, as you rush to take off your shoes and empty your pockets, you can't help but replay some of the day's events in your head. It's tough not to focus on all the back-to-back problems you encountered. You find yourself getting upset with the electric company for not being able to deliver consistent, uninterrupted service and frustrated at the rubbernecking commuters who slowed down traffic. And let's not even get started about the airline and its dysfunctional boarding pass system. The only thing that seems left to do is to wonder why this sort of thing always happens to you.

But what if we throw a twist into this getting-to-the-airport scenario? What if the person involved wasn't you but your coworker? *He* woke up late for the flight. *He* got stuck in traffic. *He* came dangerously close to missing his flight. Hearing his story, would your reaction be the same, blaming the external circumstances? Or would you wonder to yourself why he allowed himself to get so worked up? After all, his delays could have been prevented in the first place if he'd been more prepared. It would've been smart, you reason—at least in your own head—to use his cell phone as an extra fail-safe alarm clock. Or why didn't he print his boarding pass the night before? If he'd listened to the traffic report on his car radio, he could've learned about the accident and chosen an alternative route.

Here's the exact same scenario and the same set of circumstances, but we are more willing to shift perspectives when we analyze someone else's behavior. That's because psychologists have found that we apply a double standard when it comes to attribution. When it comes to ourselves, we tend to attribute good things to our own actions (take credit for them) and attribute bad things to bad luck or to external events. When it comes to others, we do the exact opposite. We usually attribute good outcomes to external factors—luck, family background—and bad ones to the individual. We do this instinctively to protect our self-image. But we pay a price in that we sacrifice our internal limelight.

Of course, as we've noted, some people are more extreme in how they view the world than others. Remember Rotter's experiment, in which participants never took any blame or credit regardless of the circumstances? Or the client who could not accept that his actions had led to his improved condition? Some people find it impossible to internalize responsibility, even for good things. And apparently that was true of Rotter himself.

In what has to be the greatest irony in psychological history, Rotter never managed to accept responsibility for his pioneering insights into the locus-of-control construct. He kept trying to distance himself from his greatest contribution to psychology, unable to understand why his discovery had received so much attention. "Naturally, I rejected luck as an explanation," Rotter reflected, but then he theorized that the popularity of the construct might have had to do with "the Vietnam War, Watergate, the inner-city riots, and political assassinations." He later dismissed those explanations as well, but he remained displeased that none of his other ideas, which he considered to be better, were "greeted by a chorus of huzzahs . . . as [was] the [locus-of-control] publication."

If the father of locus of control wasn't able to fully in-ternalize his discovery, how can we possibly shift the direction of our own limelight? One strategy is to develop sensitivity to external-oriented perspectives. Just as a wine connoisseur de-velops an instant aversion to anything with a less-than-sublime taste, we can learn to cringe whenever we find ourselves using George Costanza–like logic. Instead of focusing on how others have wronged us, we can ask ourselves, "Where am I in all of this? What responsibility can I take moving forward?" This doesn't mean that we should absolve others from responsibility. It simply means that no matter what happens, in the end the only person we have full control over is ourselves.

But when we're feeling frustrated in the moment, it's difficult to reframe the situation and attribute responsibility to ourselves. That's because when we get swept into an external perspective mind-set, we regress to thinking like children. We become fixated on how things should've been done differently *by others* and how everything would've turned out differently if everyone involved had only done what they were supposed to. Of course, attributing events externally robs us of the drive we need to effect change and navigate ourselves out of adversity. But, as we'll soon see, if you can stay focused on the immediate and realistic options that are open to you, you can transform even the most extreme of situa-tions into meaningful experiences.

3

Meaning Making

Flying over enemy territory, Major Rami Harpaz spotted a Russian-made antiaircraft missile headed directly toward his Phantom fighter. The Israeli air force pilot, returning from a war of attrition mission deep inside Egypt, was suddenly himself a target. Harpaz knew that his plane couldn't outrace the missile, but he had a trick up his sleeve: he would execute a maneuver reminiscent of a Serengeti chase. "The technique," Harpaz explains, "was to change direction abruptly, after having waited for as long as possible"—in other words, waiting to change course until just before the missile was about to strike the aircraft. Like a gazelle trying to evade its predator by pivoting at the last possible moment, Harpaz's plane swerved out of the missile's path just as it was about to strike.

The avoidance maneuver worked like clockwork, and the missile shot past the Phantom. But Harpaz wasn't in the clear yet. Only six seconds later, he spotted a *second* missile. This time, though, the Phantom didn't have enough airspeed to escape. The plane suffered a direct hit. With the tail shattered, the aircraft spun out of control.

Harpaz had only a few seconds to eject from the plane before a third missile struck, destroying the plane. But because the

Phantom was spinning so furiously, he needed to exert a tremendous amount of physical force in order to pull the ejection handle. Fueled by a surge of adrenaline, Harpaz somehow mustered the strength to pull the handle and escape from the smoke-filled cockpit. A moment later he was parachuting over foreign terrain.

In less than a minute Harpaz had gone from flying a sophisticated Phantom jet fighter at supersonic speed to helplessly hanging in the sky with no real plan. Scanning the horizon, he figured his best chance of survival would be to head for the hills once he hit the ground. But he had no chance to carry out his plan; Egyptian ground forces intercepted him as soon as he touched down.

Harpaz had to come to grips with the fact that he was now a prisoner of war. It's not uncommon for captured soldiers to pin their hopes on their eventual release. In this difficult situation, the mind naturally drifts to a better, more optimistic future, calculating how long the wait will be before freedom is regained. But there's a catch: focusing on your release date results in concentrating on events outside of your immediate sphere of influence, and inevitably you end up externalizing your limelight. The more time you spend locked up, the more you realize how little power you have and the more desperate your situation feels.

Sensing the danger of such thinking, Harpaz instinctively came up with an ingenious and creative plan. It would prove to be his most successful maneuver yet, one he had not picked up from his military training. His plan would end up not only influencing his time spent in captivity but also reshaping the course of his life.

Instead of trying to guess when others might rescue him or

negotiate his release, Harpaz made a conscious effort to focus on himself. What could he do, given his current situation, he wondered, to improve his condition? That's quite a challenge when you're locked up in a cramped Egyptian prison cell in solitary confinement. After much consideration, he came up with a plan. He'd implement a physical regimen by running four miles every evening in his cell, in tiny figure eights. And when he wasn't working out, to keep his mind engaged, he devised different mental challenges for himself, such as identifying as many prime numbers as he could between one and one thousand. The mathematical exercise served no practical purpose—after all, there's not much a POW can do with a list of prime numbers—but taking on the challenge meant he was keeping engaged and taking charge of his life. It took Harpaz two days to finally complete the task and identify all 168 different prime numbers.

The more challenges Harpaz set up for himself, the more creative he became. One day, on a whim, the pilot decided to create a makeshift garden in his cell. He extracted cottonseeds from his mattress and planted them between the concrete cracks. Another challenge he gave himself involved adding a self-reflective component to his jogging workout. As he ran his four miles daily inside his cell, he methodically delved into his past. "I decided to reconstruct my life history as I was jogging," Harpaz recalls, "go[ing] from age to age, following my school years, extracting the most detailed recollections from my mind." He left no stone unturned: "Rami the lonely kid, the rebellious teenager, the overactive young man never giving a thought to himself." Harpaz's psychological self-inventory helped him to better understand himself and has stayed with him to this day. "Since then, I know myself and can't use excuses anymore."

Rather than allowing himself to become a victim of his circumstances, Harpaz turned his time in captivity into a physical and psychological personal growth experience. That's not to ignore the many ordeals he had to endure over the years as an Israeli military prisoner in an Egyptian jail. But the challenges that he took on became the focus of his limelight. They provided him with an added sense of meaning and purpose in what would have otherwise been a barren captivity.

It turns out that this desire for generating meaning in all aspects of life is one that is common to tunnelers.

In the last chapter we saw how people who are able to overcome adversity do so by adopting an internally directed limelight. By viewing life this way, tunnelers are able to take charge of their lives. They put themselves in the driver's seat, so to speak. The question is, where do they go? The answer lies in our ability to derive meaning out of the events in our lives. An essential aspect of the drive to persevere and overcome the odds, it turns out, involves the extraction of meaning. Longitudinal studies comparing individuals who have faced adversity and overcome hardships with those who have succumbed to life's difficulties show that one of the differentiating variables is the ability to find meaning in life even under the most difficult of circumstances. Tunnelers actively seek meaning, whether in spirituality, in close interpersonal relationships, or through taking on meaningful work.

All of us can point to aspects of our lives that we consider meaningful. But tunnelers go that extra step. They place a high premium on being able to engage in activities they find fulfilling. Like Major Harpaz, during times of adversity they seek out and create meaningful experiences, sometimes out of the most mundane of things.

But what exactly do we mean when talking about "meaning"? Up until recently, empirical researchers looked upon meaning making as a phenomenon too abstract to be scientifically investigated. The entire topic seems, at first, to be more befitting a philosophical or spiritual investigation than a scientific one. But partly due to findings emanating from studies on adversity, researchers have begun looking into the nature of meaning. What role does meaning play in our well-being? What are the ramifications on our physical health? What does it mean to have a meaningful career? What can we learn from other cultures about leading a meaningful life? And, most important for our purposes, what role does meaning making play when we're facing challenging times?

Before we begin to try to answer these questions, I'd like to ask you to picture the type of researcher you believe would study the area of meaningfulness. What type of image pops to mind? You may have thought of someone resembling a sensitive psychologist or a thoughtful sociologist. Chances are you weren't thinking of an economist. Yet two prominent researchers in this area are business school professors J. Stuart Bunderson of the Washington University at St. Louis and Jeffery A. Thompson of

Brigham Young University. The two researchers stumbled across the subject of meaningfulness serendipitously, as they were attempting to solve a perplexing economic mystery.

Generally speaking, the more education a person receives, the higher his or her salary tends to be. After all, no matter what reason students provide for their decision to attend college—enriching their knowledge of the world, meeting people from diverse backgrounds, or just enjoying the college experience itself—there's always at least *some* financial incentive involved. College students expect that their degrees will open up new opportunities and offer better prospects in the job market. That's why Bunderson and Thompson became intrigued when they spotted a countertrend that defied any logical economic reasoning. And it manifested itself at, of all places, the zoo.

Amid the exotic animals and hordes of children, zookeepers easily blend into the background. Operating behind the scenes, they're responsible for carrying out the grueling work of keeping the zoo running: cleaning up filthy cages, dealing with problematic animals, ensuring proper feeding protocols. Every day zookeepers undertake a host of exhausting chores to keep the animals and visitors happy. "You go home," laments one zookeeper, "and you're absolutely exhausted and you don't feel like doing anything. It's a backbreaker."

A zookeeper's profession is regarded as so unappealing, in fact, that one non–farm animal caretaker (as they are officially classified by the government) inadvertently found himself the unwitting target of a nun's admonishment. The nun was leading a group of schoolchildren through the zoo when she spotted a zookeeper as he was performing one of his labor-intensive tasks. Quick on her feet, the nun seized the moment to teach her students a lesson. "See," she pointed directly at the zookeeper, "this is the kind of job that you get when you don't finish your education!"

But the nun was wrong. Although a zookeeper's job is difficult and demanding and the salary is meager (the average zookeeper makes around $24,800 a year), the zookeeping field is rife with college graduates. "In spite of the apparent lack of economic and status/advancement incentives associated with zookeeping," Bunderson and Thompson point out in their study, if you want to win the right to wash cages and deal with grumpy animals, you usually have to "volunteer for months or years before securing a position." Contrary to what the nun assumed, the overwhelming majority of U.S. zookeepers—82 percent—hold a college degree. The irony, as Bunderson reflected in an interview, is that the zookeeper whom the nun singled out as an uneducated laborer had more years of education than she did.

This leads us to the discrepancy that the two business school professors were trying to resolve: why would anyone who's worked so hard to earn a college degree decide to pursue an arduous, oftentimes demeaning job that pays so little? There are no hidden benefits, to be sure. It's not as if zookeepers toil for years and pay their dues and then become eligible for a higher-paying position. Nor can they transition within the industry. If you decide to become a zookeeper, that *is* your career (although many zookeepers are forced to take on an extra job to pay the bills). As one zookeeper summed it up, "Quite frankly, you give up a lot to be in the animal field. I'm not going to be rich. I'm not going to get a major award, and I'm not going to be on parade someplace." Upper mobility in the profession, moreover, is virtually nonexistent. "Most zoos," Bunderson and Thompson inform us, "offer few opportunities for hierarchical advancement beyond head keeper (a team leader who adds some supervisory responsibilities to animal care duties in exchange for a small pay increase)." As another "non–farm animal custodian" put it, "I make as much as someone at McDonald's does."

This is what Bunderson and Thompson didn't understand. Why do zookeepers do it? What makes capable college graduates compete for a low-paying, backbreaking career that most of us would be thankful to avoid? One possible explanation is that this is a sign of the times. During difficult economic periods, individuals in search of work are willing to compromise and secure jobs that they normally wouldn't pursue. But the trend in highly educated zookeepers was going on for years, well before the recent economic downturn. Besides, even when the job market is terrible, college graduates can still land better jobs working at a retail store or in an office than resorting to work as a zoo custodian.

Given the physical hardships, lack of pay, and poor career prospects, Bunderson and Thompson were confounded by zookeepers' decision to settle for the job. When they analyzed their results, they came up with a finding that surprised the business-minded pair. It turns out that zookeeping is a calling. As one animal caretaker articulated, "It's a part of who I am, and I don't know if I can explain that. When you use that expression 'it's in your blood,' like football coaches and players can never retire because it's in their blood. Whatever my genetic makeup is, I'm geared towards animals." Another zookeeper explains, "There's not much that they could do to get me to quit." And yet another says, "I can't think what would cause me to leave."

The term "calling" came up time and again in the interviews Bunderson and Thompson conducted. Zookeepers love everything about the zoo: being around animals, participating in the environmental awareness and preservation programs that modern zoos run, seeing the children's delighted reactions to the animals. In essence, they're willing to take nearly a 50 percent pay cut (the average college graduate makes about $46,000 a year) to follow their hearts in an occupation that's filled with personal meaning.

Most of us tend to think of work in less exalted terms. On a good day we say we like our job, and on a bad day we admit we can't wait for the weekend to arrive. But the sociologist Robert Bellah looks at work from a completely different perspective. He breaks down the nature of work into three distinct categories. The first is what Bellah calls merely a job. It serves as a means to an end, a way of making money. Most people's first exposure to work—waiting tables, delivering newspapers, taking orders at a fast-food chain—was a job. The easiest way to judge whether your work is a job or not is to imagine what you would do if you were to win the lottery or inherit a substantial sum of money. Would you still show up for work? If the answer is a resounding "No!," your work is likely just a job.

But if you hesitated in answering because, although the prospect of retiring is attractive, there's something about your work that you value, then your work or occupation is a career. Whereas a job has only monetary value, a career carries personal and professional attachments. It helps give us our sense of identity. We can look back and see how both our career and our life have evolved. A career is an important part of who we are.

But a career is different from a calling. A career can be intellectually satisfying. A calling is something that we are passionate about, that gives our life meaning. Think of the zookeepers. No amount of money would deter them from continuing with their work at the zoo. Maybe they'd be more selective about their hours or some of the specific chores they performed, but they couldn't just walk away from the zoo entirely. When an occupation is a calling, it becomes an inseparable part of who we are, of how we see ourselves.

But a calling is a tricky concept. As we can see in the case of the zookeepers, what may seem like drudgery to one person can be another person's passion. Think of the challenges Major Harpaz set himself during his time in captivity. Would you feel the same sense of triumph and exhilaration that he experienced by identifying prime numbers? Maybe not. But for Harpaz, those activities meant everything. They meant freedom and confirmation that he controlled his thoughts and his inner life. Most important, it's something that he actually enjoyed and in which he found meaning. Whatever our own calling might be, most of us don't tend to think about it in terms of work. The clichéd question that children are asked, "What do you want to do when you grow up?," implies a career choice. From a meaning-based perspective, it makes more sense to ask instead, "What are you most passionate about? What is your lifelong dream?"

Organizational researchers have found that employees who describe their work in terms of a calling have higher self-esteem and experience less anxiety than their career- and job-oriented counterparts. Zookeepers may live on a tight budget, but they look forward to going to work when they wake up in the morning. On the weekends they eagerly await Monday. The knowledge that you're spending your time doing what you love helps in persevering, or tunneling, through the difficult aspects of life. It's no wonder, then, that the more meaning our lives have, the less depressed we're likely to get.

But meaningfulness does more than merely provide a psychological boost. A study published in 2010 reveals the unexpected and powerful role that meaning plays in our lives. A research team made up of physicians and psychologists tracked a large group of healthy older adults over the course of seven years. At the very beginning, the scientists asked the participants to complete a battery of tests and assessments in order to collect data about them—their educational background, their cognitive functioning, the number of friends they have, any psychological issues they might have. One of the inventories that the team of scientists included was a scale that measures meaning in life. The questionnaire included items such as "I have a sense of direction and purpose in life" and "I feel good when I think of what I have done in the past and what I hope to do in the future," as well as

"I used to set goals for myself, but that now seems like a waste of time." (The first of these two statements indicates meaning; the third one indicates a lack of meaning.)

Over the ensuing years since the participants completed their initial surveys, a small but significant percentage of the elderly participants have developed Alzheimer's disease. To their surprise, the researchers found that they could look at the answers to the meaning-in-life questions that the participants had filled out years earlier to predict which individuals were likely to develop severe cognitive disabilities later in life. The degree to which the participants endorsed statements such as "I enjoy making plans for the future and working them to a reality" and "I am an active person in carrying out the plans I set for myself" reduced their likelihood of developing Alzheimer's, dementia, and other pathological cognitive deficiencies.

What's remarkable is that the differences are huge. If you take a person who scored in the bottom tenth percentile on the meaning-and-purpose survey (i.e., someone who reported experiencing very little meaning) and compare that individual with someone who scored in the upper tenth percentile (i.e., someone who reported experiencing a lot of meaning), the lower-scoring senior citizen was *two and a half times* as likely to develop Alzheimer's than his or her higher-ranking counterpart. Although we think of Alzheimer's as chiefly a biological disease that's governed by genetic factors, the level of meaningfulness in our lives plays an important role in determining whether we succumb to this illness. Regardless of gender and cultural background, the researchers found, meaning in life influences one's risk of developing Alzheimer's across the board. Even when the team controlled for other possible influences, such as "depressive symptoms, neuroticism, social network size, and number of chronic medical conditions," the connection between Alzheimer's and degree of meaning remained strong.

An equally fascinating part of the results is what happened to the majority of the participants who did *not* develop Alzheimer's. When the researchers looked only at the healthy participants, those who had earlier reported leading more meaningful lives showed less rapid rates of cognitive decline. That is, a meaningful life affected the cognitive functions of all the participants, even those who did not develop pathological disorders. As the years passed, the gap in cognitive impairment between those who experienced meaning and those who did not grew even wider.

The obvious question, then, is how can we maximize meaning in our lives? It's an inquiry that Colorado State university psychology professor Michael F. Steger was pondering even before he decided to become a psychology professor. "When I was younger," he told me when we spoke, "I remember thinking that so much of our daily activity doesn't seem to have any *point,* and I really wanted to find out what are those things that matter." His early musings turned into testable research hypotheses when Steger became the director of the Laboratory for the Study of Meaning and Quality of Life at Colorado State University.

"What we've found is that there are two ways of creating a meaningful life," Steger explains. One way is to surround yourself with meaningfulness in your life, whether it's through close family ties, volunteering your time and knowledge, or finding a career that's a calling. But even if your current work is not exactly your passion, focus on anything in your life that engages and inspires you: cooking a special meal, going on a bike ride, catching up with an old friend, singing or playing music, making a difference in someone's life. We tend to forget about the power of all the little things that bring meaning into our life.

"But that's just one way of having a meaningful life," Steger explains. "The other way is to find the right question." Here's what Steger means by that. Think back to a time in your life when you were unsure about something. Perhaps you were uncertain about which college major to pursue or what career path to follow. Or maybe your uncertainty involved accepting a position at another company or questioning the value of a friendship or the validity of a deeply held belief. What was that time like for you? Did it feel exciting and liberating? Or was it something that weighed you down?

If you're like most Americans, you do your best to avoid uncertainty. "There seems to be something about our culture," reflects Steger, "that the more you're searching for meaning, the less happy you look." When we find meaning, we're content, and that contentment reveals itself in the way we come across and the way we feel. But when we're searching for meaning, we're much more likely to be anxious or depressed. Steger's research shows that our reaction to lacking meaning in our lives only gets worse with age.

It's one thing to be a confused teenager wondering about the meaning of life. That's not atypical. It's much more disturbing if you're in your twenties or thirties and still unsure about your prospects. Chances are you're unhappy. "Especially after college," Steger explains, "it seems like there's an acceleration in the magnitude of the relationship between how much people are searching for meaning and how much distress they're reporting." In other words, we can tolerate uncertainty when we're young, but if we haven't found meaning later in life, we feel there must be something wrong. These fears grow progressively worse with age. Older Americans, Steger cautions, are especially vulnerable. "If you're sixty-five or older and you're still asking the question 'What's the purpose of my life?,' there's a pretty good chance you're also experiencing depressive and anxiety symptoms."

Steger's findings are significant when we consider the implications of the times when we face adversity. When life is at its most tumultuous, that's when we often lack a sense of meaning. Without meaning in our lives, we experience even more distress, aggravating the situation and creating a vicious cycle. But it doesn't have to be that way. As Steger explains, "Some of the cross-cultural research we've done suggests that 'searchiness' is actually a positive thing in some places." In Japan and Korea, for example, "you don't get the anxiety and despair associated with the process of searching." That is, whereas Americans and other Westerners appear to feel uncomfortable when they're searching for meaning, individuals in other cultures derive meaning from the search itself.

Why the substantive cultural difference? At least partly because in the United States we equate certainty with meaning. As we grow older, we expect to find our place in the world. We expect to know who we are and what we want out of life. Any major life transition—a career shift, a relationship breakup, a landmark birthday—can cause us to reevaluate what is truly meaningful for us, creating discomfort and anxiety. But in cultures such as Japan and Korea, exploration and personal growth are valued as lifelong pursuits. Meaning seeking is not looked upon as a deficiency. Pondering the meaning of life and what path you want to take is appreciated as an important and meaningful activity in and of itself. What if Westerners were open to the Japanese and Korean concept of continuously seeking meaning? Steger explains that questions such as "What am I most passionate about?," "What can I do to make sure I'm living my life to the fullest?," and "What's most important to me?" could serve as lifelong emotional indicators that point us to greater meaning.

The ramifications are significant. Take someone who has lost his job and is going through the breakup of a marriage or relationship. Dealing with career and relationship uncertainty, an individual can easily start to doubt the meaningfulness of his life. "Everything I thought was certain is now gone." But if we reframe the same situation from a meaningful search perspective, the situation can actually be experienced as liberating. The opportunities are all open. "Now I have a chance to look for the right person to be with." It can be approached with a real sense of excitement.

Up to this point in our investigation, we've looked at meaning largely from the perspective of an individual. But pursuing meaning doesn't have to be a purely solitary endeavor. To what degree do our normal, everyday interactions with those close to us affect our meaning-making abilities? Monisha Pasupathi and Ben Rich, psychologists from the University of Utah, set out to explore how our interactions with others and the meaning we derive from them affect our ability to derive joy from simple tasks.

The psychologists recruited sixty pairs of real-life friends to participate in a clever experiment. The pairs, whose friendship averaged 5.6 years, were randomly split and separated. One member of each duo was asked to spend fifteen minutes in the lab playing The Sims, a character-driven life-simulation computer game. The actual content of the game had little to do with the experiment; Pasupathi and Rich focused on what the participants got out of the game. Did they enjoy playing it? Was it fun? When the researchers asked the game players about their experience, most of them reported generally liking the game. On a scale of 1 to 6, participants rated their enjoyment of the game, on average, as 4.

While their friends were evaluating the computer game, the remaining participants received a separate task. The researchers divided them randomly into three groups and asked them to act in one of three specific ways in response to their friends' sharing of the experience of having just played The Sims. A third of the friends received the easiest task. Their instruction was to simply be attentive and engaged, acting the way they normally would during a friendly conversation.

The second subgroup was asked to take on an antagonistic stance. They were told to be disagreeable and continuously shoot down their friend's assertions, poking holes in their friend's opinions. Pasupathi and Rich predicted that players whose friends pooh-poohed their experience would unconsciously reconsider just how much they had really enjoyed the game.

The third and final group of friends was given the hardest task, to disengage entirely. That's more challenging than it may first appear. It's difficult to tune out someone for a long period of time. Think of all the times you've been sitting in a restaurant, trying to mind your own business, but you just couldn't help pick up bits and pieces of the conversations around you. Now imagine listening to a close friend talk about a fun activity and forcing yourself to completely zone out—for the entire conversation. It's possible to allow our attention to drift for a few moments, but to keep at it for fifteen solid minutes is virtually impossible. In fact, during trial runs Pasupathi and Rich conducted before the actual experiment began, they found that none of the volunteers could remain zoned out continuously; people inevitably reengaged.

The research pair realized that they had to come up with an inventive solution in order for the experiment to work. Fortunately, they hit on a creative fix. Instead of instructing the participants *not* to pay attention to what their friends were saying, they asked them to carefully and methodically count every single "th" utterance their partner made. If the game player said, "One of the things I liked about The Sims is that . . ." the friend's inner dialogue would go, "One of the—one—things—two—I liked about The—three—Sims is that—four." This finally did the trick; the participants were so focused on the trivial task that they appeared completely oblivious.

After conversing with their friends, all sixty players from

the three groups were asked once again to rate their level of enjoyment of the game they had played earlier. Pasupathi and Rich wanted to see what effect, if any, the game players' interactions with their friends had on their earlier experience. When the psychologists analyzed the results, they discovered a curious pattern. As expected, the group of friends who had played the game and received positive, confirmatory feedback from their counterparts maintained their original enjoyment scores. That is, when the researchers asked them how they liked the game after they conversed with their friends, they provided virtually identical marks to those they had given previously, right after they finished playing.

But contrary to Pasupathi and Rich's predictions, the group of game players who received a *negative* reaction from their buddies remained similarly unaffected. Their postconversation game-enjoyment scores were just as high as the original evaluations. Despite their friends' contrary opinions, those game players liked the game just as much.

The real surprise came when the researchers looked at the last set of participants, those whose friends had reacted in a detached manner. Instead of listening to their friends' experience, this group, as you recall, simply counted the number of "th" sounds they emitted. It turns out that the friends' indifference made a big difference to the game players. Their postconversation game-enjoyment scores dropped significantly. When asked how they felt about the game after encountering their disengaged friend, they labeled their experience as being just average.

How do we make sense of the results? If we look at the

data from a meaning-making perspective, the first two conditions (receiving affirmative feedback or contradictory feedback) stirred up meaningful discussions. Even when the friends appeared to be at odds, they were still engaged, and their conversation was lively. The game players received feedback and food for thought while holding on to their subjective experience. After all, just because your friend disagrees with you, that doesn't mean that your own subjective experience was lessened.

We might expect that the indifferent group would result in the *least* amount of change to the level of enjoyment. After all, the disengaged friends allowed their game-playing buddies to talk without challenging them or interfering with their reactions. They neither reinterpreted nor questioned their friends' evaluations. But apathy, in the form of a close friend who just doesn't seem to care, took a toll on the players. Like a deflating balloon, the conversation, or lack thereof, sapped the enjoyment that the game players had initially felt. They began to downgrade their own subjective evaluation of their earlier game-playing activity.

Meaningful interactions are especially important during difficult times in our lives. As a psychologist, when I work with individuals struggling with sadness, loneliness, or depression, I find that oftentimes their condition is associated with a lack of meaning in their lives. But they're rarely aware of it. They know that they're feeling down, that they cry too often or easily, or that they're not as engaged in life as they once were. But they can't quite put a finger on why they feel as they do. Like most of us, they don't actively gauge or monitor the level of meaning in their lives. Bringing meaning back into their life through engagement in therapy, finding a fulfilling job, forming a significant relationship with a loved one, and even connecting with a small group of friends capable of intimate, caring conversations can alleviate many of the original symptoms.

The most common mistake that most of us make when it comes to finding meaning in life is that we think big. We wait and hope for a transformational moment to shake us up and change the way we live, such as a near-death experience that suddenly reorganizes our priorities. But that's just one way to develop meaning in our lives. There's another, more powerful way—by focusing on the small things in life. This takes us full circle back to Major Harpaz, the Israeli fighter pilot. Instead of waiting for a big "Ah-ha!" moment to strike him, he found meaning in self-exploration and nurturing a makeshift cotton seedling "garden."

Eight weeks into captivity, Harpaz's routine changed drastically. He was transferred to a bigger holding cell with nine other prisoners of war. After two months without any contact with fellow Israelis, Harpaz appreciated the company. But in a strange and intriguing way, it made his time in prison more challenging. His fellow cell occupants spent the bulk of their time the way most prisoners do: waiting around, with no real agenda. "They lived without an ideological pivot or focus which might have organized their lives," Harpaz remembers.

The major, who already knew firsthand about the vital importance of meaning making, realized that if he didn't want to lose his inner drive, he'd have to change the group dynamics. For starters, Harpaz, the highest-ranking officer in the group, suggested that they all adopt a democratic system in which everybody had an equal voice and each contributed to the well-being of their small community. They convened for weekly formal meetings to discuss everything from food rationing to what name to give the stray cat that wondered into their quarters from time to time. The discussions often became heated, but, as Harpaz explains, the important thing wasn't necessarily the actual content but being engaged and having a stake in how things turned out. Just as in The Sims experiment, apathy destroys meaningfulness.

Weekly meetings, of course, are not enough to break the monotony of imprisonment. Following Harpaz's lead, the men decided to actively infuse meaning into their everyday routine. They founded their own college, of sorts, where different soldiers took turns teaching the others what they knew. Lessons began at exactly nine every morning. The prisoners could take physics, math, English, geography. "We were successful in creating a way of life. We didn't just sit and stare at the ceiling and ask: 'When will the time pass? What do you do now?'"

Once their classes ended for the day, they spent the rest of their time on collaborative projects, such as building an Eiffel Tower replica with matches. "We all occupied ourselves with calculating the measures and proportions," Harpaz explained. Other projects included a book club. They would choose a book, read it, and discuss it. Harpaz alone read more than three hundred books during his time in captivity, "More than I read in the ten years before or after." The group even took on the Herculean task of translating *The Hobbit* into Hebrew. "Coping with Tolkien's English was a challenge," Harpaz recalled. "We tried to convey the atmosphere and the spirit of the story, and this raised our creativity to its climax. . . . The four months dedicated to this project was a beautiful period, full of elation; it gave us a sense that we were winning against the whole world." Later, when the hostages were freed, the manuscript was published; it stands today as one of only two Hebrew translations of Tolkien's work.

The meaning-making projects were so consuming that one of Harpaz's fellow captives found it difficult to let them go. As he reflected years later, "At the end, after three years, when they came to inform us that in three days we'd go home, I said in my heart, how can I leave now? There are so many things I'm in the middle of doing! I had plans for two weeks more."

Within the horror-filled walls of the Egyptian prison, Harpaz and the other captives constructed their own utopian world filled with meaning. Reflecting on their time together, one of the soldiers remembered, "I got to know myself better in captivity." Another appreciated the "family-like relationship we developed in jail." Even the college they created came in handy. Many of the soldiers' math and English skills improved tremendously. "I learned subjects I would have never been exposed to otherwise, and I read a lot," explained one of the group members. The entire experience transformed adversity into something meaningful. "It may sound horrible," admitted one of the former detainees, "but my time in captivity helped me a lot in life. . . . Today I can cope with any problem that may come up, as difficult as it may be."

When we immerse ourselves in meaningful activities, however minor or symbolic they may appear to us at the time, we significantly improve our odds of flourishing in the face of adversity. "The biggest thing we learned from captivity," Harpaz said, summing up his group's experience, "is that from every starting point, one has the possibility of climbing up or falling down, and it's a matter of choice which it will be." By embracing that internal limelight stance and striving to capture every little morsel of meaning we can from wherever life might take us, we nurture the drive on which tunnelers rely.

There are three important takeaways here. The first is that we should search for meaning in the significant aspects of our lives: our careers, interactions with loved ones, and friendships. In times of adversity, when meaning is lacking, it's especially important to seek meaning from the small things in life: reading, dancing, hiking, making art, watching a good movie. And it's important to remember that the search for meaning is just as valuable and can be just as satisfying as discovering meaning. To see this in action and learn about the third and last component of the drive to succeed, we turn to a spirited, independently minded woman who repeatedly ignored every bit of sensible advice she ever received.

4

Unwavering Commitment

Ruth Jones graduated from high school in 1914 during an era when women had few career opportunities. "I had to earn my living," she explained, "but I didn't want to be a nurse, I didn't want to be a nun, I didn't want to be a teacher, I didn't want to be a secretary." Identifying what she *didn't* want to do was easy, but when it came to choosing her career, she felt stuck. There was nothing that grabbed her interest. Things changed dramatically when a school friend casually invited her to attend a local, small-town matinee play with her. Sitting up in the balcony, gazing at the stage, she became transfixed by the abilities of the actors. This, she realized—acting—was her calling. It was a surprising revelation. In fact, she faced any number of serious challenges that would put a damper on any aspiring actress's enthusiasm: "I wasn't pretty," she reflected, "I was five feet tall, I didn't know anyone on the stage, I didn't know anyone in New York." And if that weren't enough, she didn't know the first thing about acting and had no money to live on.

If Jones had come of age today, with a wider range of career options available to her, she might more easily have come to terms with reality and pursued a more down-to-earth career track in show business, one that would have fit her qualifications better. But faced with only the traditional options—nun, teacher, secretary, nurse—versus her dream of becoming an actress, Jones didn't have to think twice about it. She enrolled in the American Academy of Dramatic Arts and convinced her parents to cover a year's tuition—no small sum. It required her mother to take out a loan on her life insurance plan and her father to cash in his savings account. With so much of the family's resources invested in her education, Jones put everything she had into her schooling. And at the end of her first year of studies, the president of the school asked her to have a word with him. It was obvious that she was a dedicated student, he told her, but "we don't think you're suited to the stage." In case Jones didn't quite get the message, he quickly added, "Don't come back."

When you consider the context of the times, you have to hand it to Jones for persevering with her dream. She was a young woman who refused to conform to society's expectations. She declined to settle for a job or career she knew she would hate or get married because that was the only other viable option. But what could she do now? She'd already spent a year of her life and much of her family's savings on acting school. To continue acting would be quixotic, if not outright pigheaded. By her own assessment, she didn't have what it took to break into the industry. She had given it all she could; maybe acting wasn't in the cards for her. When even your acting teacher thinks you have no future in show business, it's probably time to call it quits. But something in Jones just wouldn't let her give up. She was determined to pursue her passion with everything she had, and she wasn't about to stop now.

So Jones moved to New York City, changed her last name to Gordon (formerly her middle name), and spent her days going from audition to audition. If she could land a role even as an extra, she reasoned, at least it'd be *something*. "Long days of job hunting," she remembered, "trying to get to be an actress through August, September, October, now it was cold November 1915." One wet and miserable winter's day, Gordon entered Billy Shine's Movie Extra Agency, hoping to land her first break.

What happened next not only shaped Gordon's career, it also provides us with a valuable insight into the minds of tunnelers when they find themselves in a bind. When Gordon walked into the office, she found herself in a jam-packed room filled with wannabe actors, all vying for parts as extras. Over the past several months, Gordon had visited dozens of places like it, an office in an old building catering to dreamers who'd give their right arms to be in the movies. On this particular day, Billy Shine, the head of the small agency, needed two hundred extras to play the parts of guests attending a posh party. "In 1915," Gordon explained, "if you had a ball gown and worked as an extra, it paid five dollars!" Gordon badly needed the money, but, more important, she needed a break. She eagerly watched Billy Shine scan the roomful of hopefuls, as he pointed in different directions at those he thought were believable enough to make the cut. As usual, Gordon wasn't selected.

Although she was disappointed—by now she was no stranger to rejection—Gordon saw a glimmer of an opportunity. The aspiring actress figured she might as well show up at the shoot anyway. "Don't give up," she told herself, "go to Murray's Hanging Gardens at seven [A.M.] and bring a ball gown. Wouldn't somebody oversleep?" Two days later, dressed in a fancy gown, Gordon was on the set, trying her best to look the part and blend in with the two hundred other extras who were there. When Shine realized she had arrived without having been invited, he confronted her. "Did I engage you?" he asked her. Gordon explained that she was there in case he needed a substitute. Instead of appreciating her thoughtfulness, Shine became enraged. He yelled at her at the top of his lungs, "*Out!* Get the hell *out!*" He continued yelling at her, adding a final threat: "I'm personally gonna see you never work *again!*"

Gordon was horrified as she made her way through the hall toward the exit. "Two hundred pairs of eyes watched me carry my suitcase across the dance floor." Shine's threat was still echoing in her head. Being humiliated in front of two hundred aspiring actors marked a new low. No one would've blamed her if she decided to quit. Instead, she searched deep inside herself for any kernel of strength she could muster.

Ruth Gordon's ordeal triggers one of two completely different reactions. Hearing her story, either you're rooting for her, or you hope she finally gets the point and moves on to pursue something else. The way you lean says more about you than you might think, according to the research of Dr. Suzanne Kobasa.

When Kobasa was still a graduate student in the University of Chicago's Behavioral Sciences program, she came up with a clever doctoral dissertation research question that no one had bothered to ask before. Health care professionals have known for decades that there is a link between emotional stress and physical illness. That is, if you experience a stressful life event (e.g., losing your job, moving, getting divorced), your chances of developing physiological symptoms increase. But not everyone who endures difficult life transitions becomes sick. And Kobasa wanted to know why. What differentiates those who experience stress and come down with symptoms from those who face similar obstacles but remain healthy?

In order to find out what forces are at work, Kobasa needed a large enough sample of people who experience stress on a regular basis. What a better group to look at, she reasoned, than middle- and upper-level executives? The young researcher obtained permission from a large company giving her full access to its managers. Kobasa interviewed them, asking them to relate every recent stressful event that they had encountered. She also wanted to know about their general health, their personality, and the attitudes they had about life. Once Kobasa collected all the data, she focused her attention on the executives who reported the highest levels of stress. She then split the executives into two groups: the ones whose physical health remained strong despite their taxing life events and the ones who succumbed to an illness. In what crucial ways, Kobasa wondered, would these two groups differ?

This is where things get very interesting. When Kobasa analyzed her data, she discovered a pattern that'll sound uncannily familiar. The qualities that differentiated Kobasa's healthy executives from the ones who became sick are the same characteristics we have been exploring so far in our investigation. That is, the healthy managers adopted an internal limelight orientation and relied on meaning to shape their lives. Although Kobasa looked at highly functioning executives confronting stress rather than embattled individuals struggling with adversity, she arrived at the exact same findings. The psychological characteristics that help successful managers tunnel through their difficulties are the same qualities that allow youngsters from disadvantaged backgrounds to overcome theirs.

Kobasa's research, though, did much more than merely replicate what we already know about tunneling. Her investigation uncovered a new insight into the attitude of tunnelers. Kobasa noticed that the executives who fared well under stress were more relentless than their peers, staying the course even during difficult times. For tunnelers, Kobasa explains, "the encounter with a stressful environment is mitigated by a sense of purpose that prevents giving up on one's social context and oneself in times of great pressure." In other words, because tunnelers place themselves in situations that are rife with meaning, they find it easier to stay true to their goals even in tough times. Unwavering commitment helps tunnelers persevere through situations that overwhelm most other people.

This relentless quality fits Ruth Gordon to a T. No matter what obstacles she encountered in her pursuit of acting, she did not give up or succumb to negativity. Even when Billy Shine banished her from the movie set, she refused to throw in the towel. It's not that Gordon wasn't shaken up by the event—was Shine serious, she wondered, about carrying out his threat to destroy her career? Had she really been that out of line for showing up uninvited in case they needed a substitute? But she didn't allow that experience to derail her passion for acting. And that's where tunnelers are different from most of us. Throughout this difficult period of her life, Gordon's commitment to pursuing an acting career never wavered. Quitting wasn't something she considered. "Things had to get better," she reasoned. "They *had* to! Even on that horrible morning I *believed* it."

From a purely rational perspective, Gordon's analysis of the situation is more sound than it might at first appear. Many of us would feel dejected and call it quits. But think it through. Why let Billy Shine—a casting agent for extras—be the person who determines your career path? Just because Gordon's plan to show up as a substitute backfired, that was no reason to give up. She'd known the odds were against her when she showed up at the set. She'd given it a good try, and it hadn't worked out. Instead of allowing her emotional state—feeling hurt, rejected, discombobulated— dictate her next move, she was able to stay focused. She didn't get caught up in the emotional drama. And as we'll see shortly, this ability to avoid an emotional roller coaster plays an important role in tunnelers' relentlessness.

Gordon eventually succeeded in getting herself cast in a film later on that year—albeit as an extra in a little-known movie called *The Whirl of Life*. But it marked her first success. And in the following years she steadily built a strong acting career on Broadway. Despite it all, though, Billy Shine's words hung like a curse around her movie career. She didn't land a single film role for the next twenty-five years. It wasn't for lack of trying. Whenever she auditioned for a part, the assessment of the directors was strikingly the same: "She acts all right, but you can't photograph her." Gordon, true to her tunneler's mentality, kept at it. If casting was where she was getting stymied, she figured, maybe she should stop showing up at auditions altogether. She figured that eventually someone would like her stage acting well enough to offer her a role on the big screen without needing to test in front of the camera. And in 1940 somebody did just that. She was invited to play Lincoln's wife in *Abe Lincoln in Illinois*—her first film acting role.

Gordon was in her seventies before she finally got a chance to prove Billy Shine completely wrong: she won an Academy Award for best supporting actress for her role as Minnie Castevet in *Rosemary's Baby*. Reflecting on her career and her determination, Gordon offered words of advice that could only come from a tunneler: "Never give up; and never, under any circumstances, no matter what—never face the facts."

It's an outlook shared by the late senator Paul Wellstone. Up until 1990 Wellstone was an ordinary citizen, working as a professor of political science at Carleton College. But that year one of Minnesota's Senate seats was up for grabs. Well, sort of. Republican senator Rudy Boschwitz had occupied the office since 1978. The incumbent was up for reelection, and for all intents and purposes his reelection bid was just a formality. Boschwitz enjoyed a 71 percent approval rating, strong name recognition, and a political career free of scandals—a popular incumbent who had the full support of his party and Minnesota voters.

Boschwitz was so heavily favored to win the race, in fact, that no serious Democratic contenders bothered to throw their hats into the ring. Why waste time campaigning against a shoo-in who basically already had a lock on the election? Only someone who had nothing to lose would take on the challenge. Enter Paul Wellstone. His candidacy surprised everyone, even his closest friends. Wellstone was a virtual unknown. His only other foray into politics had taken place eight years earlier, in 1982, when he had lost the Minnesota state auditor election in a landslide.

Boschwitz was so comfortable with his prospects that he didn't even bother campaigning for the race. The two candidates were in completely different leagues. Boschwitz was a two-term senator, and Wellstone wasn't even a politician. On both the local and national levels the reelection was regarded as nothing more than an exercise in democratic protocol.

Wellstone was the only one who didn't buy in to that view. Like Ruth Gordon, who passionately pursued acting because she found it so meaningful, Wellstone was enamored with the notion of serving in the Senate. He had a strong populist agenda, and he wanted to make a real difference for those lacking a voice in politics. Never mind that he had no political experience and that he was running against a seasoned political heavyweight.

Wellstone was such a long shot, in fact, that even his own party didn't take him seriously. One of the key requirements of any aspiring politician is money. Wellstone received very little of it.

The Democratic Party, for one, didn't want to throw good money away on a race the Republicans already had in their back pocket. And not many other contributors lined up to support Wellstone. As a result, not only was he an underdog, he was an underfunded one. It would've been bad enough if Boschwitz had had twice the campaign funds of Wellstone. But the incumbent outraised his opponent by a staggering five-to-one ratio.

Imagine being in Wellstone's place. Nobody knows you, and you're up against an established politician who's well liked and heavily financed. Your party doesn't seem to care about the race, and your campaign bank account is seriously lacking. If you're like most people, you'd likely resign yourself to the facts and figure that, hey, at least one day I'll have a good story to tell my grandkids.

But not Wellstone; he took the race seriously and played to win. "We knew from the very first minute we met him," remembers one of Wellstone's few financial backers, "that he had the energy and passion to carry it through to completion." Working within the limits of his budget, Wellstone bought a used school bus that would've better served a hippie tour band than a politician. He rode in the eyesore bus—painted green—throughout Minnesota, drumming up support wherever he could. The little money he had left over went toward the purchase of television spots. In one of them, he briefly introduced himself to the voters before apologizing that "unlike my opponent, I don't have six million dollars, so I'm going to have to talk fast." The camera quickly pans from shot to shot as Wellstone tries to keep up with the rushed timing of the ad by quickly blurting out one-sentence summaries of his environmental goals, his connection to the farming community, and his health care ambitions. You feel exhausted just watching the commercial.

Boschwitz kept his distance. He didn't want to have anything to do with his pesky competitor. A public debate, of course, was out of the question.

Wellstone used this to his advantage. Instead of taking Boschwitz's snub as an insult, he relentlessly pursued him for a chance to debate. But the incumbent senator was nowhere to be found. Wellstone pursued every route he could—attempting to reach Boschwitz by leaving messages with his campaign team, trying to locate him in person, even calling the operator to get his number. Wellstone documented his efforts and aired a two-minute documentary-style ad about his futile search for Boschwitz.

Wellstone's creative efforts garnered him increasing attention, and he started to make headway in the polls. Seeing that his challenger wouldn't quietly go away, Boschwitz finally agreed to a debate. But it proved to be too little, too late for the incumbent. Wellstone's momentum pushed him ahead in the polls as he achieved what had seemed impossible just a few weeks earlier. Wellstone won the seat by a margin of less than 3 percentage points. He was the only political challenger that year to throw out an incumbent from the Senate.

Tunnelers don't always succeed in their endeavors, of course. For every Ruth Gordon and Paul Wellstone trying to make it, there are thousands who follow their dreams without fully attaining their goals. But even when tunnelers fall short of their expectations, their unwavering commitment has its own inherent value. Even when they don't achieve their goals, they keep moving on and making progress. The process of taking on challenges, weathering hardships, and committing to the outcome makes them stronger in the end.

Although as an aspiring actress and an aspiring politician Ruth Gordon and Paul Wellstone pursued completely different career paths, both embodied a tunneler's drive: They relied on themselves as agents of change, refusing to allow naysayers to dictate their destiny. They passionately pursued their calling, even when everything seemed to be going against them. And they doggedly pursued their ambitions, believing in themselves and never allowing thoughts of failure to deter them.

As the psychologists Frederick Rhodewalt and Joan B. Zone found, tunnelers process information differently from most people. Building on Kobasa's research about individuals who have overcome adversity, Rhodewalt and Zone interviewed hundreds of individuals, collecting information about their personalities, attitudes, and life experiences. Do tunnelers encounter as many difficult life experiences as normal individuals do? the researchers wondered. When the psychologists examined the results of their study, they found, interestingly, no difference in the number of hardships tunnelers and others encountered. That is, tunnelers are just as likely to experience tough situations as the rest of us. But there was a significant difference in the way they *perceived* adversity.

When the researchers asked the participants to rate the level of desirability of each challenging life event they had encountered, nontunnelers "declared that roughly 40% of their life experiences were undesirable." Tunnelers, on the other hand, "appraised only 27% of their experiences in such a manner." The differences between the two groups become clearer when we consider the array of life experiences we all go through. If you mapped out your life history, you could easily identify life experiences filled with positive memories: interactions with friends, getting married, the birth of a child, memorable vacations, time spent with loved ones. There are also events that anyone would categorize as negative: the death of somebody special, going through a divorce or breakup, losing one's job, encountering serious health issues.

But there are also plenty of experiences that fall into something of a gray area—events that can be viewed as either positive or negative, depending on your perspective. Take moving to a new location. Is that positive or negative? Some would look at a move through the lens of adversity (being uprooted, leaving old friends behind, having to get used to a new neighborhood or city). But one can just as easily see the experience as positive (exploring a new city, making new friends). It is in the realm of those ambiguous life situations that tunnelers are more prone to see the positive. It's a lot easier to stay the course when a potential obstacle (e.g., being chewed out by a casting director or being ignored in a political race) is viewed as a challenge or learning experience (*How can I prove them wrong?*) than a scarring experience (*I'm just not cut out for this*). The way in which we interpret such gray-area life events can have lasting effects on our life.

Because tunnelers have a tendency to view obstacles as challenges, psychologically speaking, they experience fewer disappointments in life, resulting in less fatigue. Life doesn't take as heavy a toll on them. That's one reason they have an easier time staying committed to their goals when they run into obstacles. Rhodewalt and Zone found that nontunnelers are about *three times as likely* to develop psychological (e.g., depression) or physiological (e.g., flu) symptoms in response to a tumultuous life event.

Tunnelers find it easier to stay the course because they gravitate toward meaning; they're more likely to perceive a potential obstacle as a challenge than as a setback; and their psychological and physiological reactions are more robust. This sense of relentlessness is more than just perspective and attitude, though. It's linked, as it turns out, to a fundamental feature of personality.

In the very early days of personality psychology research, a theorist by the name of Gordon Allport attempted to come up with a psychological periodic table of sorts. Just as chemists were able to identify and assemble the elements, Allport wanted to construct a similarly cohesive system for classifying personality traits. Born and raised in the Midwest, Allport prided himself on being thorough and practical. He decided to take a straightforward, no-nonsense approach to his project. He opened the dictionary and, together with a colleague, sifted through tens of thousands of words, writing down all the adjectives he could find that described personality characteristics: sensitive, attentive, cunning, passionate, gregarious, altruistic.

After months of work Allport and his partner had compiled

a list of roughly 18,000 such words. His next step was to combine words with similar meanings and reduce the list to a more manageable 4,500 adjectives. But this was still a far cry from creating a useful, compact list of core personality traits. The task was just too overwhelming for Allport to carry out.

Only decades later, when computers became widely available, could psychologists use them to make further headway with the personality classification task. With computers, psychologists could identify clusters of words that described similar underlying concepts. The personality list quickly dwindled down to a much more manageable sixteen items. And by the 1980s psychologists were able to distill the core personality traits down to just five. Interestingly, psychologists from completely different disciplines and theoretical orientations somehow independently arrived at more or less the same five key elements. It's as if a diverse group of members of Congress offered their ideas on how to best reduce the federal deficit and at the end of the day they all arrived at the same five concrete steps. Psychologists are notorious for disagreeing with one another—after all, psychology is not an exact science—so when the field as a whole settles on something as challenging as what makes up personality, it's a pretty significant (and rare) step.

So what are the five core personality traits? The first is *extroversion*. Extroverts, as most of us know, enjoy interacting with others, while introverts, at the other end of the construct pole, prefer sticking to themselves.

Another core trait is *agreeableness,* the seeking and valuing of interpersonal harmony. Agreeable people are conflict-averse, tactful, and empathic. They're not very competitive and think of others before they think of themselves. Here's a quick and easy test to see where you fall on the agreeable scale. If you were a manager in a company and learned you would have to fire an employee, how would you feel about it? Would you feel anxious, concerned about how to best deliver the news to the person in a way that would be as painless as possible, or would you think, "Hey, business is business, this person just no longer fits our needs"? An agreeable person would have a harder time letting someone go than someone who did not score highly on the scale.

The extroversion and agreeableness scales are similar in that both have a social, interpersonal component to them. They determine the way we interact with others. Generally speaking, the more extroverted and agreeable you are, the more easily you'll be able to build social connections and maintain a support system. As we'll see later on in our investigation of tunnelers, having the right type of social support is a key component that helps tunnelers make it through difficult times.

One of the most interesting core personality traits, and perhaps the most difficult one to fully articulate, is *openness to experience*. This characteristic has to do with being creative, reflective, and able to think abstractly and see connections and patterns even among things that don't seem to be related. Individuals who are open to new experiences gravitate toward art, aesthetics, and new ways of looking at things. If you read this paragraph and it makes perfect sense, this probably is you. If it leaves you puzzled, then chances are you prefer things that are more concrete and down to earth. You are more likely to value tradition. Either is fine. This is one personality trait that is not related in any way to overcoming adversity.

The fourth major personality trait is *conscientiousness*. Individuals who score highly in conscientiousness tend to be responsible, goal-oriented, and achievement-minded. They are self-disciplined go-getters. They may not be as spontaneous as others, but they know how to develop a plan and stick to it. Conscientiousness is an invaluable quality of tunnelers; it helps them stay on task.

But it is the fifth trait that matters the most when it comes to the relentlessness tunnelers possess. Do you tend to worry about how things will turn out? Do you take things personally, or are your feelings hurt easily? Are you frequently overwhelmed by stress or anxiety? Would you describe yourself as moody? If you answered "no" to most of these questions, you have an *emotionally stable* personality. The opposite of that is neuroticism.

Neurotic individuals are more fragile and more easily become hurt and upset. They tend to have a consistent negative self-script running in their heads. They criticize themselves to the point that they come to believe the harsh opinions they have of themselves, internalizing them as part of their self-identity. Look at Ruth Gordon's response when she was thrown out of the movie audition, and Paul Wellstone's attitude when everyone, including his own party, treated him as a joke. It would have been easy for either of them to get down on themselves: *What was I thinking? I*

*shouldn't have attempted that. What's the point of continuing to pur-
sue this?*

Even when Gordon and Wellstone might have been self-
critical, they didn't allow that neurotic narrative to become their
dominant voice. That's the key difference between tunnelers and
those who succumb to adversity. The criticizing voice acts as an
extra strain that can undermine our tenacity. Instead of ruminat-
ing on their failures and blaming themselves, Wellstone and Gordon focused on their passion and its meaning in their lives. After
all, that was what brought them to make the commitment they
did in the first place.

I've noticed, working as a psychologist, that my clients become more comfortable with following through on their plans
when their self-concept and self-talk shift from critical to accepting. They find it easier to take risks and ask someone out whom
they'd normally be hesitant to approach, apply for jobs that are a
couple of notches higher than their current levels, or express their
opinions even when they think they may not be popular.

Up until now we've looked at what motivates or drives tunnelers.
How do they shift gears and change the course of their apparent destiny? As we've seen, it's not that they somehow manage
to avoid running into obstacles. Instead, they find ways of side-
stepping them. They're able to accomplish this, in part, by seeing
themselves as responsible for their fates and futures. Most of us
vacillate between an internal and external locus of control; when
we feel we've been wronged, we focus on the injustice that was

done to us. Tunnelers, even when they are not responsible for the hardships they encounter, hold themselves accountable for handling the situation. And when it comes to considering choices and alternatives, they're attracted to the conditions, relationships, tasks, and events that are rife with meaning. Most people think of meaning as a positive by-product of the things we do, but tunnelers make meaning a priority in their actions and lives. Because they have a sense of purposefulness, they find it easier to hold on to their goals and aspirations during tough times. Instead of playing a negative self-script in their minds every time they hit an obstacle, they view the obstacle as a challenge to be overcome. These are the key drivers behind how tunnelers maneuver out of their disadvantages and upbringing. But what about the orientation that tunnelers embrace in life? We start by exploring the similar temperaments shared by a college softball player and an Iraq War combat survivor.

ORIENTATION

5

Temperament and Success

No one expected much of the University of Georgia women's softball team when it kicked off its 2009 season. The Lady Bulldogs were especially young—all but two of the players were underclassmen—and besides, Georgia had never once made it to the Women's College World Series in its school history. But the team had a hidden advantage of sorts—an elusive, intangible quality that researchers have spotted over and over again in tunnelers.

Playing shortstop for Georgia that year was Kristin Schnake, one of only two seniors on the 2009 squad. Schnake stands only five feet tall, looks young for her age, and has a fun-loving, spunky energy. Born and raised on a farm in Illinois, Schnake wasn't groomed to be a collegiate athlete. In fact, she wasn't originally slated to be a starter, as she struggled to find her footing on the team. "I was the backup for a lot of positions," she explained, "taking balls in the outfield, just ready for anything." Only when Schnake was a sophomore did her hard work and persistence finally pay off, earning her the starting shortstop position.

Georgia surprised everyone in 2009 when it started off the season with a 13–1 record. Without any obvious standout stars on the team and without much experience under their belts, somehow the Bulldogs managed to come together as a team. They kept on winning games, and by season's end they had achieved what earlier in the year seemed impossible: they had earned their way to the coveted World Series. Never mind that they entered the postseason event as underdogs. For them, just getting there was a huge accomplishment.

The young team got off to a shaky start, though, in the World Series, losing their very first game to one of the top contenders, the University of Washington. Fortunately for the Lady Bulldogs, the double-elimination format of the tournament meant that Georgia was still alive. But they couldn't lose another game. During the next two matchups, Georgia breezed by Missouri 5–2, and just when it looked as though they were going to be eliminated during their next game, they came from behind to beat Michigan 7–5.

Georgia's run in the World Series was surprising. None of the players had any postseason experience, and the Bulldogs had no obvious star players. But what was equally surprising was the way in which Schnake and the Bulldogs carried themselves on the playing field. One would expect a team of relatively green players to be nervous and intimidated or stiff and overly eager, but the Bulldogs appeared unusually relaxed.

They played their games with the laid-back style and attitude of a weekend game with family and friends on a sunny afternoon cookout. Imagine having so much fun that you high-five your teammates every chance you get, roll your eyes and shrug your shoulders when a close call goes against your team, and playfully strike a favorite dance pose whenever you hear music play-ing in the stands. Well, that's exactly the way the 2009 Bulldogs played in the World Series—all engineered by Schnake.

The senior shortstop was having the time of her life. She celebrated with her teammates after they made even the most basic of plays. Schnake delivered so many "attagirl"s to the pitcher after nearly every pitch that the umpires were forced to delay play. "If Christie's [the pitcher] kind of lulling there," Schnake ex-plained, "I come up and say, 'Come on, we're going to get this girl. We have your back; there's all eight of us here. You're not the only one on this mound.'" When Schnake herself made a play, she'd pound her chest like Tarzan, her signature display on the playing field. And in between innings, when the Beach Boys' "Wipeout" played over the loudspeaker, Schnake jumped on her air surfboard and led her team in a series of '60s dance moves. It's almost as if she didn't realize she was playing in the most important softball tournament of her life.

Some of the experts covering the game didn't take to the Bulldogs' antics. But Schnake wasn't doing it just for kicks. She refused to allow the pressure of the situation get to her or to the team. Whenever she noticed her teammates tensing up, she'd quickly remind them to take it easy. "I just tell them," Schnake explained, "'It's just softball; it's all it is. We might be at the World Series, but all it is is a softball game.' . . . I just try to keep them calm and loose and excited and wanting to play."

It was exactly the type of worry-free play the young Lady Bulldogs needed. As the tournament progressed, the Georgia players continued to play relaxed, have more fun, and cheer each other on. Schnake herself fed off of her team's high energy. She hit five home runs in the World Series, after hitting only one home run in her previous 204 games.

The Georgia Bulldogs Cinderella story continued as the team made it to the semifinals, where they once again faced the University of Washington—the team they had lost to in the opening round. Washington took an early 3–0 lead, but Georgia continued to play loose and relaxed. They didn't allow concern at being behind in this critical game cripple their playing style. With their positive, fun-loving attitude, they scored three runs to tie the game. Shortly after, Schnake celebrated the biggest moment in her softball career—she hit a three-run homer. As she rounded third base, she stretched her arms out wide like airplane wings, advancing toward her high-fiving teammates awaiting her at home plate. Washington rallied back, but the Bulldogs squeaked out a 9–8 victory, handing their opponents their first loss in the tournament. Because Georgia had come into the game with a loss and Washington had been undefeated in the double-elimination tournament, the two teams would have to play each other again later in the afternoon to determine which team would make it to the finals.

But beating Washington back-to-back—in the same day— proved to be too tall an order for the young Bulldogs. They fell behind early, and, down 9–3 late in the ninth inning, it was clear that their run in the World Series—as grand and unexpected as it was—was near its end. Looking at Schnake, though, you would have thought the Bulldogs were winning. She continued to exude the same spirited attitude, cracking jokes, laughing, and goofing off with her teammates. For her, it was a once-in-a-lifetime experience, an achievement no one had expected from the young team. And Schnake wanted to relish in the moment as much as she could. Although the Bulldogs were losing, she didn't let it dampen her mood. After all, her team deserved credit for making it that far, handing Washington, which went on to win the World Series that year, its only tournament loss.

Schnake's attitude is about more than just good sportsmanship. As the New York University psychiatrists Alexander Thomas and Stella Chess attest, having an *even-tempered disposition* plays an important role in achieving success in our lives. The pair of psychiatrists first came up with their findings when they observed the behavior of infants. Most of us think of babies as being very much alike: they cry, sleep, eat, and test themselves and the world around them. But Thomas and Chess noticed some important differences among the infants. It all came down to temperament. The psychiatrists identified three distinct types of personalities among the babies: difficult, slow to warm up, and easy. The infants with a difficult temperament tend to be fussy and restless. They cry frequently and are hard to console (think of a crowded airplane with a baby that won't stop screaming). The slow-to-warm-up infants are shy and take time to adjust to new people and unfamiliar situations. The easy-temperament babies, in contrast, are usually content and in good spirits. They seem to go with the flow, without becoming discombobulated or upset by the world around them.

But here's the really interesting part. When Thomas and

Chess tracked a cohort of babies over time, from childhood to adulthood, they discovered that the general temperaments that individuals exhibited as infants remained with them throughout their lives. It's an astonishing notion to consider: the way we approach the world as infants foreshadows the way we will approach life as adults. The fussy baby who won't stop pouting is on track to become the adult who won't stop complaining. And the happy-go-lucky infant is likely to turn out as a mellow grown-up.

Before we continue, though, it's important to note that temperament is not fixed in stone. We can all learn to achieve an even temperament if we work at it. A calm disposition serves as a kind of protective psychological shield against depression, obstacles, and adversity. Easygoing people are less likely to let stressful events upset them or get them down. Think of how you react to bad news or frustrating circumstances. Do you take life as it comes, without getting irritated or upset, or do you find yourself getting easily worked up?

Longitudinal studies that look at how people handle adversity over time have found that an even-tempered disposition is one of the qualities that separate tunnelers from their counterparts. At first glance, an easy temperament may seem to be counterproductive to success. After all, we normally think of successful individuals as having a type A personality, those who push ahead forcefully and relentlessly. But tunnelers tend to be relentless in their drive while being easygoing in temperament. Like Schnake, they can be highly committed and focused while still maintaining an enthusiastic orientation to life.

Previously we saw the importance of the drive that enables tunnelers to pull themselves out of harsh circumstances. Equally imperative is the orientation tunnelers adopt in response to the life situations they encounter. When it comes to dealing with challenges and obstacles, having an easy temperament drastically shifts the way we experience life.

Of course, it's one thing to exhibit an easy attitude when playing a softball game. But what about when the stakes are much higher? Perhaps nothing speaks more clearly of the power and effectiveness of an easy temperament than a soldier in the midst of combat. For retired major David Underwood, his temperament made a life-changing difference. As the son of an air force officer, Underwood spent his childhood years moving from place to place. "I was born in Oklahoma," he told me, "and four weeks later we moved to the Philippines." Before enrolling in high school, Underwood had lived in West Africa, California, Virginia, and Vietnam. But instead of being bothered by the constant relocation, he had a relaxed view of it all. "I got exposed to different cultures and met people all over the world."

Underwood dreamed of following in his father's footsteps, planning to enlist in the air force. But his less-than-perfect eyesight prevented him from becoming a pilot. "If I couldn't fly airplanes," he reasoned, "I might as well jump out of them." Underwood joined the army and spent a year in Baghdad in 2005. His tour, considering the locale, was relatively calm. "I didn't have anybody actually shoot at me," he remembers. But things were different during Underwood's second deployment to Iraq in May

2007. The U.S. military surge was just getting under way, and Underwood and his five-hundred-man unit were placed twenty kilometers south of Baghdad, in what was supposed to be a quiet and remote location, away from the hotspots.

Underwood's battalion was one of several units that were strategically located around Baghdad to keep the city secure. Their job was to prevent al-Qaeda and its insurgents from infiltrating the metropolitan area. But military intelligence underestimated the significance of Underwood's location. His unit was positioned in a prime spot with easy access to three roads and a bridge, all leading into Baghdad. Strategically speaking, if his men were successful, the enemy's access to the Green Zone—the center of the international presence in Baghdad—from the south would have been highly restricted. Few people, including Underwood himself, anticipated the amount of resistance that al-Qaeda would put up in response to the blockade.

"No one saw it coming," Underwood explains. "We were supposed to be there just under a month, so I rolled in with minimal force." From the very first day, Underwood and his men were under fire. "We had a hundred and forty-five attacks launched at us the first six weeks I was there." Every evening, as the sun went down, the unit endured a continuous barrage of mortars, machine-gun fire, rocket-propelled grenades, improvised explosive devices, and sniper attacks. "You name it, they were shooting it at us."

Six weeks into his deployment, Underwood learned that al-Qaeda had posted a $60,000 reward on his head. A few weeks later, the bounty had doubled to $120,000. Underwood experienced many near misses and caught more than one lucky break. "I was surprised that I was still alive," he recounts. In January 2008, eight months after his arrival in Iraq, Underwood was conducting a routine mission in a nearby deserted village. He was zigzagging his way on foot through empty houses often used by the insurgents as bomb-making factories. The reason Underwood was there was to personally check for any signs of life, to ensure that there were no civilians present, before he ordered his unit to detonate the houses. "I didn't want to hurt or kill anybody I didn't have to."

All of a sudden Underwood heard a loud blast and everything turned black. An improvised explosive device located in one of the house's windows had gone off. "Next thing I knew," he recounts, "I was about ten feet away, on my back, in thick black smoke. I'm lying there. My left arm is buzzing, like it does when it falls asleep."

Despite the shock of the blast, Underwood remained alert. "My first two reactions are that I can still think, which means the explosive didn't hit me in the head. And the second reaction is relief because I'm alive." But Underwood realized that he hadn't survived the blast unscathed. "I looked down, and my leg is messed up." And when he looked at his tingling left arm, he saw that it was crushed below the elbow. It was clear even then that it would have to be amputated.

Underwood had managed to evade the attacks targeted against him for months, only to be knocked out by a crudely constructed booby trap in the middle of nowhere, intended for no one in particular.

But instead of getting worked up about his misfortune, he accepted his plight with a positive attitude. "I have heard the guys who are bitter and upset, sitting there going 'Why?'" he reflects. "I never asked, 'Why?' I was like, 'Wow! I can't believe I lived through that shit.'"

He underwent twenty-five surgeries to repair his arm and leg. Yet his spirits remained high. "They were ready to take me to yet another surgery—I had a surgery every other day—and my commanding officer was there. He said, 'Are you okay?' and I answered him honestly, 'Yes, sir, I'm fine, it's just an arm, I'm okay.'"

Underwood wasn't in denial or harboring false hope about his recovery. He saw the facts the way anyone else would. But his even-tempered attitude made dealing with adversity much more manageable. As Underwood's experience taught him, the outlook you generally carry in life determines how you deal with adversity. "Take a guy who habitually whines and complains," Underwood explains. "If he gets injured, he's still going to whine and complain. Getting blown up is not going to make you a better soldier. When you suffer a loss, it's not as if you have an epiphany and all of a sudden go 'I see the light.'" Coming face-to-face with this kind of hardship allows an individual's underlying temperament to emerge. "For me," Underwood reflects, "I became even more positive. I wanted to get things done, move forward." That's the important lesson Underwood offers: that a relaxed attitude about the small things in life makes the big ones a lot more manageable.

Instead of isolating himself and fretting over his injury, Underwood joined the Wounded Warrior Project, a nonprofit organization that advocates for injured veterans. He participated in suicide-prevention campaigns, took up physical challenges like long-distance bicycle riding, and worked to battle discrimination against the disabled. He says he has absolutely no regrets about everything he has endured, and you can tell by his voice that he means it.

Without realizing it, most of us shift our mood based on situational cues to which we've learned to respond. If we lose a competitive game, we feel upset. If we suffer a health-related setback, we feel distraught. But as Schnake and Underwood illustrate, we don't have to respond that way. The orientation of tunnelers is different; they don't react solely based on how others expect them to act. They don't let events dictate how they should feel. Their attitude doesn't change when a misfortune befalls them.

Think of the last time you received a traffic ticket or were reprimanded at work. What was your reaction? Obviously no one enjoys being in such a situation. But did it ruin your day? Did it take over your week? Or did you tell yourself, "Okay, I need to learn from this. I need to move forward"? Those who have a difficult temperament take on a rigid, perfectionist perspective to life. Their tolerance for unplanned and unpleasant events is low. Bad news paralyzes them, robbing them of the flexibility needed to bounce back and successfully maneuver through hardships. This doesn't mean that we should never get upset about anything, of course, or that we should mask the way we feel. Having an even temperament doesn't mean being a zombie. But it means not overreacting to situations. People with even temperaments do get concerned and frustrated at times, when appropriate. But that's not their default mode. Their natural tendency is to remain calm and positive.

Looking at Underwood and Schnake, we see that their easy temperament helped them stay calm and positive, even when dealing with physical and emotional losses. Obviously, Underwood's injury was more significant and emotionally overwhelming. But the point is that the way we deal with the small things in life helps determine how we'll react to the bigger events, as well. When we don't let the small things get to us and we focus on getting the most out of life, we essentially train ourselves to remain calm under pressure. When individuals who think that way encounter a more difficult situation, they are in a much better position to take things in stride, instead of becoming unraveled.

For eBay CEO John Donahoe, the importance of temperament first became apparent when he was a first-year business school student at Stanford. Donahoe, in his early twenties, was newly married, and the couple was expecting their first child. The delivery date, though, fell during finals week of the first term. With so much to juggle—starting business school and preparing for a baby—Donahoe figured there was no way he could devote as much time and energy to his studies as he would've liked. "I showed up with an excuse of why I didn't have to do well," he recalls. In addition to learning new material, adjusting to the expectations of the professors, and networking with his cohort, Donahoe was loading up on baby supplies and helping his wife through the last stages of her pregnancy.

Fortunately for Donahoe, Stanford's Graduate School of Business had a student-friendly pass/no pass grading system. That meant Donahoe didn't have to worry about his GPA. All he needed to do to get credit for a course was to obtain a P−, the lowest distinction necessary to pass. A few students who performed above expectations received a P+. Most received a P. If you truly excelled you received an H, signifying "honors." Donahoe said to himself, "I'm like, 'I'm having a baby. It doesn't really matter. I don't have to do well.'" That took a lot of pressure off the young father-to-be. Instead of being stressed-out and tense, like most incoming students, Donahoe could tackle his workload feeling relaxed. To his surprise, he aced all of his five courses—"I got five Hs that fall term," without even meaning to. Donahoe realized that he performed at his best when he was operating with an even-tempered attitude.

That first-term experience in graduate school came in handy to Donahoe more than twenty years later when he became the CEO of eBay in 2008. The entire corporate world was feeling the pain of the financial crisis, but eBay was in worse shape than most. Its core auction business had stalled; its stock was in free fall; and, in a very real way, it was on the edge of disaster.

Back in the early days of the Internet, when online commerce was still new, people had flocked to eBay to bid on virtually anything they fancied. But by 2008, with thousands of online stores selling brand-new merchandise at a discount, the novelty of purchasing other people's used stuff had worn off. On top of that, eBay had made some questionable decisions, such as acquiring Skype. To many financial analysts, eBay was a fading star whose only hope for future growth was to be acquired by a larger company.

Donahoe knew that if eBay was going to turn things around, it needed to change. He started planning ways to divest the company of Skype. He trimmed down eBay's workforce to make it more efficient. And, most important, he shifted the focus of eBay away from online auctions to its online payment-processing unit, PayPal, and fixed-price marketplace sales (the "buy it now" feature). Donahoe's decisions made sense from a business perspective, but the eBay faithful—especially the auction sellers—were not too happy with the new changes and direction. "It wasn't easy," reflected Donahoe. "I had hate videos about me on You-Tube." In one of them Donahoe was depicted as a Nazi officer from *Schindler's List* shooting a prisoner who stood for eBay.

But as in his early business school days, the more chaotic the situation around him became, the calmer Donahoe was. This is exactly what eBay needed in a leader, someone who could stay collected under pressure. Donahoe tried to make peace with his critics and learn from anyone who cared to voice practical suggestions. Through it all, Donahoe kept his cool and maintained his even-tempered demeanor. Instead of getting upset, he spent time writing reflectively in his personal journal. He relied on his family to keep him grounded. "They don't care about my title, they don't care about any perks of power. They care about am I being authentic, do I have integrity?"

Under Donahoe's leadership, eBay made a turnaround and

regained its stride. Its stock price increased threefold from 2009 to 2011. And what did Donahoe learn from leading a company in a time of great turmoil? "All I can tell you as you go on in life is, crisis happens. It happens to yourself, it happens to your family, it happens to your kids. And I think one of the things we learn to do is to embrace it because there is so much that comes out of it. And it makes you a better person and a better leader."

The scientific research supports Donahoe's view. A pair of Australian psychologists found that even young children were able to benefit from an even temperament during trying times. Jan Smith and Margot Prior followed thirty-two families that had experienced several major life stressors (e.g., unemployment, chronic illness, poverty, poor housing, poor interpersonal relationships). Each family had endured at least two "major life events that had a negative impact." The psychologists were especially interested in how the children had dealt with the hardships. How were they faring developmentally, given their challenging life situations? Smith and Prior interviewed the parents, teachers, and children, collecting as much psychological data as they could.

As a group, the children were more likely to act out and experience psychological problems, as well as social difficulties, compared with other children their age. But not all the children fit the pattern. A large segment showed no behavioral or social deficiencies. They did well both at home and in school. The psychologists wanted to find out what situations or characteristics accounted for the children's ability to persevere. Smith and Prior found that the quality of the mother-child relationship, the presence of a father at home, above-average intelligence, and low stress levels all contributed to a child's ability to tunnel through adversity. But the most consistent variable that contributed to a child's behavior at home as well as in school and his or her ability to integrate socially was an easy temperament. As the authors explained, an even-tempered disposition "was easily the most discriminating variable in the analysis."

What can we do if we're not one of those individuals born with an easygoing temperament? Although we can't expect an infant to alter his or her orientation toward the world, as adults we have the power to adjust or choose how we react. When we're faced with losses or difficult situations, do we allow ourselves to become, metaphorically, the wailing baby on the airplane—complaining about what's going on, getting worked up, and feeling frustrated? Or do we take time to appreciate the things that are going well for us?

The challenge in adopting an even temperament is that there's a natural fear in us that if we don't get all worked up, we'll lose control of the situation. It's as if we tense up in preparation for the looming catastrophe. But that very reaction, ironically, gets in the way of our efforts to deal successfully with the obstacle.

Our orientation toward the world determines the way we experience hardships and react to them. The solution might be as simple as finding levity in an otherwise somber situation. As a group of study participants about to experience the greatest shock of their lives found out, there's more to the power of humor than meets the eye.

6

Humor Counteracting Adversity

In 1990 a team of three psychologists from Allegheny College, a small liberal arts school in Pennsylvania, ran an experiment that held a surprise for each of its fifty-three participants. Most psychological studies follow a simple protocol: participants arrive at the laboratory, fill out questionnaires, and then perform some mundane tasks on a computer, interact with other participants, or complete a cognitive skills task. But sometimes the stakes are much higher.

In the Allegheny study, each of the subjects arrived to meet a research assistant who sat him or her down next to a large digital screen and proceeded to fit the student with electric shock receptors. You can imagine the thoughts that raced through the participants' minds as they questioned their decision to sign up for the study. Once fitted with the electrodes, the subjects received a set of important instructions. The digital monitor in front of them, they were told, would display a timed countdown, starting at twelve minutes and winding down all the way to zero. Every thirty seconds each participant would be prompted to report his or her anxiety level on a scale of 1 to 10. The electrodes, the instructions revealed, were there for a reason. When the clock reached 0, each subject would receive a strong shock of electric current.

Why would a team of psychologists purposefully administer electric shocks to fifty-three of their own college students? Ostensibly, the participants were told, it was to test a physiological theory involving the temporal section of the brain and its reaction to shock response. That was just a cover story, but, of course, the students did not know that. Picture yourself sitting alone in front of a screen, hooked up to electrodes and bracing for a powerful electric shock. You can see how your anxiety level would inevitably start to rise. (The researchers informed the participants that they could quit the experiment at any moment for any reason without suffering any negative repercussions. But whether out of bravery or a reluctance to be viewed as quitters, none of the students took them up on that offer.)

Up until that point in the experiment, all the participants were treated identically. Everyone was hooked up to the electrodes, learned about the countdown, and mentally prepared for a less-than-pleasant encounter with an electric current. But there was a final twist. Before the countdown began, the researchers asked a third of the subjects—selected at random—to put on a set of headphones and listen to a recording of comedy acts for the entire duration of the countdown. This group of students got to spend the twelve-minute preshock period listening to a medley of stand-up routines by Bill Cosby, Steve Martin, Robin Williams, and George Carlin.

Another group of subjects, again selected at random, listened to a different recording—a passage from a geology textbook. The researchers selected the most engaging geological excerpt they could find, "a lively discussion of volcanoes and other rather interesting geological phenomena." It's safe to say, though, that as exciting as volcanoes might be, most college students, given the choice, would opt for humor over geology. Still, the geological lesson provided a welcome distraction from the countdowns and the anticipation leading to the electric shock. The rest of the students received no auditory reprieve. Left to their own devices, they simply stared at the digital countdown screen and reported their rising anxiety levels every thirty seconds.

Before the countdown began, all students displayed some initial anxiety. Those who had nothing to listen to reported, on average, an anxiety level of 2.8 on a scale of 1 to 10. The geology group averaged 2.5 and those selected to listen to comedy reported an average of just 2.0. In other words, even before the countdown started and the students began listening to the recordings, anxiety levels differed among the subgroups.

Over the next several minutes, the subjects watched the countdown, listened to their audio segment (those who were given one), and recorded their anxiety levels. The countdown clock wound down relentlessly. Nine minutes later, three minutes before the shock, the control group students' anxiety scores were already a full point higher than their precountdown levels. The geology students also reported increased anxiety. But the humor participants continued to hover near their initially low baseline rate.

Ninety seconds before the shock, the anxiety levels rose exponentially. Students who did not have a recording to listen to were now reporting an average score of 5.1. The geology folks recorded a 4.4. The humor students, remarkably, held at 2.7, not far from their baseline. That's quite a discrepancy in scores.

While the no-audio group was now reporting serious signs of discomfort, the comedy condition students were not much more perturbed than they had been prior to the countdown. Clearly the students listening to comedy were not experiencing the same level of tension and nervousness as their peers.

As the big moment was set to arrive, only a few seconds before the end of the countdown, the audio-free control group reached a new high on the stress level. Their anxiety levels shot up to 6.0. The geology students followed closely at 5.7; apparently the volcano descriptions did little to stem their anxiety. The humor participants also began to exhibit some distress, though their anxiety remained significantly lower than that of the other two groups, with an average score of 4.5.

Let's take a step back here and look at the big picture. Humor not only provided the participants with a starting advantage by lowering their initial anxiety levels, it also delayed the onset of anxiety as the countdown proceeded. It took eight full minutes for the students listening to comedy to reach the baseline anxiety levels of the geology and no-audio participants. In other words, eight minutes after the countdown commenced, the humor group's anxiety levels had reached only the *initial* anxiety scores of their peers. The comedy listeners continued to remain a healthy step behind the other groups the entire time.

As the countdown finally wound down to zero seconds left, the participants winced in anticipation. They waited for a current of electricity to run through their bodies. But nothing happened. No shock was given to them. The psychologists, it turns out, had had no intention of shocking the students. The electrodes were actually just phony props. The anxiety induced by the experiment was real, but the point was for the researchers to gather data measuring the effects of humor on stress-induced anxiety.

From a physiological perspective, scientists have long known about the positive effects of humor. You may not realize it, but when you laugh your muscles relax, your blood pressure drops, your breathing eases, and even your pain tolerance increases. The Allegheny shock experiment approached humor from a *psychological* perspective and showed the degree to which humor can shield us from the emotional impacts of unpleasant experiences. This protective property of humor applies outside the laboratory walls, as well.

Vietnam War POWs found humor to be a lifesaving tool. You'd think that under the consistent duress of captivity—worrying about survival, enduring harsh conditions, and being treated inhumanely—humor would not have been a top concern in the POWs' lives. But an organizational systems specialist, Linda Henman, found that the opposite was true. Henman interviewed former Vietnam War POWs and found that humor had played an essential role in helping them overcome their circumstances. "Several of the study participants commented that they considered humor so important," Henman explained, "that they would literally risk torture to tell a joke through the walls to another prisoner who needed to be cheered up." Soldiers realized in a very fundamental way that humor can act as a protective barrier to the effects of adversity, bolstering each other's mood and improving their psychological well-being.

One POW who spent weeks in solitary confinement remembers the day he rediscovered the power of humor to transform the travails of his day-to-day existence. He was watching his two guards through a small hole in the wall when one of them asked his partner for the time. The second guard, accommodating his counterpart's request, handed over his rifle to the first guard, took off his bullet belt, removed his trench coat, and pulled out an alarm clock from his pocket. "I'd been beaten pretty severely every day for most of a month," remembered the soldier, "and I was just absolutely rolling on the floor. . . . He didn't have a watch; he had a Baby Ben clock stuck in his pants pocket." Given the unrelieved bleakness of the POW's circumstances, the scene absolutely broke him up and, for a moment, let him completely block out his pain and sense of isolation.

Though the exchange between the guards might not strike most of us as being all that funny—after all, retrieving an alarm clock out of a pocket is not exactly the epitome of humor—it marked a turning point for the captive soldier. As a POW you learn to appreciate any moment of levity you can find. "I realized, 'I thought I was going to die today; and all I did today was have a good laugh.'" From that day forward he actively searched for humor wherever he could. "[I]t became apparent to [me] that humor was going to play a major role."

Emmy Werner, the developmental psychologist pioneer who tracked young tunnelers in Kauai, noted in her research that the children who appear to be immune to the effects of adversity also appear to have a good sense of humor. It was just a casual observation, but one child psychologist, Ann Masten, found that humor plays an important role in overcoming adversity from a very early age. Masten collected data on nearly a hundred elementary school students who attended schools in urban neighborhoods. Many of the kids lived in single-parent households that commonly faced financial hardship. Masten wanted to see whether the children with a good sense of humor had an advantage over their peers. And if humor did make a difference, she wanted to know how. Of course, measuring a child's sense of humor can be a little tricky. For that matter, measuring *anyone's* sense of humor is difficult. How do you determine who has a good sense of humor?

Masten reached for a creative solution. She collected a couple of dozen Ziggy comics and presented them to each of her young subjects. For each cartoon, Masten recorded the child's reaction (e.g., laughter, smile) and asked him or her to explain the humor behind the comic strip. For several of the cartoons, Masten deleted the caption that contained the punch line and asked each participant to provide one of his or her own. The people she enlisted as judges were blind to which captions came from the children and which ones were original Ziggys. They rated some of the children's entries as funnier than those of the original cartoon. That is, some of the children's humor was so well developed that it was on par with that of a professional cartoonist.

Masten next compared her data with information she collected about the children at school. She found that the children who displayed a strong sense of humor—quickly getting the Ziggy cartoons, coming up with the best original captions—performed better in school than the children who did not have as well developed a sense of humor. Moreover, children with better humor "were viewed by their teachers as more effectively engaged in the classroom and more attentive, cooperative, responsive, and productive." And it wasn't only the teachers who held those students in high regard. "Their peers viewed them as more popular, gregarious, and happy and as leaders with good ideas for things to do."

Why does a sense of humor go such a long way toward boosting success? Part of the reason is due to humor's anxiety-shielding qualities. Just as humor shielded the Allegheny study participants from the stress and anxiety of the countdown to getting shocked, children with a healthy sense of humor are protected from anxiety arising out of the tension and hardships in their lives. This makes it easier to engage in life and not succumb to difficult conditions. In this regard, humor serves a role similar to that of having an easy temperament. Both qualities appear to reduce the intensity and negativity associated with adversity.

But humor does more than just decrease anxiety. As she tested kids on Ziggy cartoons and performance in school, Masten noticed an interesting development. The children's observed sense of humor overlapped with their intellectual and emotional intelligence. The children who displayed a good sense of humor were also the same children who performed highly on intelligence measures. The mental sophistication needed to comprehend and appreciate humor is apparently connected to the cognitive abilities required to perform well intellectually and academically.

The same is true of emotional intelligence. Masten explains that humor requires the same "social 'know-how'" that plays an integral role in emotional intelligence. In order to produce something funny, you need to come up with clever content and deliver it in such a manner that has the right timing, awareness of social cues, and sensitivity to the audience and interpersonal dynamics.

Parents regularly devote time to helping their children improve their reading, math, and music skills, but we usually don't think of joke telling and goofing around as intelligence boosters. Not only is humor a fun and effective way to build up intelligence, it also reduces anxiety and strengthens interpersonal bonds.

Because humor protects us from the intensity of stress, it is much more than just a positive quality we normally associate with charm and wit. A highly developed sense of humor is linked to intelligence and resilience—the ability to bounce back from failure or setbacks. Unfortunately, though, when dealing with a crisis, the first thing that is usually sacrificed is humor. We tell ourselves that this is no time for levity, the situation is too serious. In fact, it may be when we need comic relief the most.

But are all forms of humor equal? In other words, are some types of humor superior to others in relieving stress? Have you ever heard a remark that you found funny but others perceived as being distasteful or offensive?

Humor is especially tricky when it's used during arguments. A team of Canadian psychologists wanted to see how humor shapes the quality of romantic relationships, particularly during times of conflict. They recruited nearly one hundred couples and asked them how they see themselves, how they feel about their partners, and what they think about their relationship. Once the researchers collected the initial information they needed, they sent the participants on their way—but not before handing out diaries, requesting that each person keep a running log of events in his and her relationship over the next two weeks. Afterward, the couples returned to the laboratory with their relationship journals in hand.

What happened next was unexpected. The researchers asked the couples to sift through their diaries and select a disagreement from the previous week that remained unresolved. If there was more than one unsettled issue, the couples were told to choose the most serious and meaningful one. After a brief discussion with their significant other, each couple settled on a topic. The researchers allotted them just seven minutes to do their best to resolve the conflict and iron out their differences. Not every couple made significant headway, of course. Immediately after their attempt, the pairs were once again separated and whisked away to different rooms. Each partner was then asked to reflect on the discussion they had just had. How much progress had they make during the short conversation? How close did they feel to their significant other?

Unbeknownst to the couples, while they were engaged in their conflict-resolution discussions, the researchers analyzed the frequency and type of humor used by each partner. The results offer some interesting insights into what happens when we argue with loved ones and people with whom we are close. The first pattern to emerge is that if one partner uses humor, the other one is more likely to join along and use humor as well. There is something infectious about humor that draws out levity in others. Humor not only eases tensions during difficult discussions but helps to forge a closer connection with the other person. When the other party senses that we're open to humor, he or she recip-rocates in kind; defenses drop away, and the entire tone of the conversation shifts. And that's exactly what happened with the "conflict resolution" couples. In many cases they used humor to ease the tension, which allowed them to make progress on their issues. The couples who used humor effectively reported feeling closer to their partner and being more satisfied with the overall relationship. They also felt that they had made progress in resolv-ing their underlying conflict.

But not all participants responded to their partner's attempt at humor. Some were indifferent to their partner's approach, find-ing the attempt at comedy counterproductive. Why would some people appreciate humor while others resented it? It all comes down to the *type* of humor used by their partners. Participants who resorted to what psychologists call *affiliative*—or essentially positive—humor tended to have pleasant interactions with their partners. These individuals added levity to break the tension, pointing out comical observations, relating funny stories, or mak-ing silly remarks. The second group of participants used *aggressive* humor, including sarcasm, cynical quips, and demeaning personal attacks. Their humor did more harm than good. Their zings and jabs might have seemed funny to them, but their observations only added fuel to the fire and soured the conversation. Their partners felt distanced and reported elevated levels of distress. Instead of their humor relieving anxiety, it added to it; instead of connecting with their partners, they drove their partners further away.

On the face of it, the solution seems simple. We should use affiliative humor to reduce anxiety and mend conflicts and avoid sarcasm and aggressive humor that threatens and alienates people. For many years the psychological community advocated this exact position. The virtues of affiliative humor were praised, while aggressive humor was regarded as mean-spirited and insensitive. Some psychologists even went as far as to label aggressive humor as a form of bullying, emanating from deep-seated emotional issues inside the person attempting to be funny.

But not everyone agrees with this position. Though it may not be wise to resort to sarcasm and put-downs when trying to resolve a conflict, couldn't edgy humor be productive in other contexts? It took someone outside the field of psychology, a communications professor by the name of Jenepher Lennox Terrion, to consider the possible virtues of aggressive humor. Bringing an anthropological fieldwork perspective to bear, Terrion immersed herself for six weeks in a midlevel executive training program for high-ranking Canadian police officers.

The officers had been selected to attend an intensive leadership training course, marking an important step in their career advancement. Candidates are handpicked from various geographical locations across Canada, meaning that they are strangers to one another when they first meet. For six weeks, they lived together on site, attending educational seminars and doing most everything else together as well. Terrion didn't have any background or experience in police work. Her goal was to see how these officers use humor to build rapport with one another.

The cohort to which Terrion was assigned consisted of twenty-seven police officers, all of whom, except for one, were male. All of them held a supervisory role in their jobs back home: most of them were in charge of ten or more officers. For all practical purposes, Terrion became part of the group, attending every educational session with them, joining them during breaks, eating meals together, and accompanying them on their recreational activities. Terrion didn't pretend to be a policewoman. She presented herself as a researcher studying "patterns of group development"—a phrase that's sophisticated enough to sound smart but vague enough to not give away anything about her real research interests. What Terrion was really there to see was how aggressive humor impacts interpersonal interactions.

Police officers are notorious for using nontraditional humor to alleviate the stress that comes with their job, as well as to enhance the tight bonds they form with one another. But would seasoned, successful police officers looking to advance on the force incorporate street humor during their training? Would the presence of a woman police officer—and a woman researcher—alter the dynamic among group members? And if aggressive humor was used, what purpose did it serve, and how would it impact the interpersonal relationships?

From the beginning of the program, Terrion observed all kinds of humor. One policeman self-deprecatingly described himself as a "goofy Newfie" (drawing on the Canadian stereotype of Newfoundlanders as country bumpkins) and told a joke in which Newfoundland was the punch line. Another officer, a French speaker, made a joke of his English skills. Quite a few participants poked fun at their profession: their low pay, lack of academic education, and even their short life expectancy after retirement.

The field of psychology has traditionally frowned upon these types of self-deprecating statements because they're thought to stem from insecurity. If you're not confident about yourself, the argument goes, you beat others to the punch by putting yourself down before they have a chance to do so. But self-deprecating humor can also signal an approachable, even-tempered, down-to-earth personality. Think of leaders you know—a boss, a teacher, a mentor—who had the courage and self-confidence to poke fun at themselves. What did you think of those individuals? Did you find them insecure, or did you appreciate the fact that their humor showed that they did not take themselves too seriously? Self-deprecating humor, if used appropriately, can reduce the social distance between two people; it shows that leaders have human faults like anyone else and that those using such humor are open to being genuine and equal with others. As Terrion explained, "self-putdowns effectively level one's status," making the relationship more egalitarian. It also serves another purpose. The officers participating in the course used self-deprecating humor "as a catalyst to establish an environment where comic interaction becomes accepted and even celebrated."

During her six-week immersion with the police officers, Terrion noticed that as the officers got to know one another better and began bonding together as a group, the biting humor escalated. When LJ, one of the group members, delivered an especially polished and well-prepared presentation, the next presenter, MJ, walked up to the flip chart and jokingly tossed LJ's paper on the floor. With mock disgust, he added, "Good presentation, guys," eliciting laughter from the entire group. Although on the face of it MJ was making fun of LJ's presentation, the pretend derision served to highlight LJ's superior skills (if LJ's presentation had failed, MJ's biting remarks wouldn't have been funny).

As the weeks progressed, the put-downs became more grounded in truth. Midway through the fourth week, as the group was being taught about different leadership styles, the seminar instructor argued that a good leader varies his or her style depending on the situational context and the subordinates involved. One of the officers disagreed with the presenter, arguing that he had not changed his leadership style "for the last five jobs I've had." Another officer seized the moment to interject, "That's why they moved you." The entire group spontaneously broke into laughter. But this put-down was different from the earlier one where MJ had poked fun at LJ's presentation. This time there was an edge of truth. Nevertheless, the group members—including the officer targeted—laughed at the quip. It served as an important sign that the group felt comfortable and secure enough to poke fun at one another. They had bonded.

Terrion's findings raise three important questions. The first one involves the "who" in negative humor. Within a group, who's usually the butt of put-downs? Do we tend to poke fun at those who are not popular or those who are held in high regard? The second question involves the "why" behind aggressive humor. Why do highly regarded professionals resort to teasing put-downs of one another? What purpose does this type of humor serve? The most important question is about the "how." How can edgy humor be helpful when dealing with situations of adversity?

The trick to a successful put-down (besides showing how quick and witty you can be) is to pick on someone you and the group truly like. When Terrion asked every officer to name the individuals in the group whom he or she liked best, she found that the less popular people were less frequently at the receiving end of a put-down. As one officer explained, "You would know you weren't part of the group if nobody ever made fun of you." Instead of put-downs being used as a vehicle for shaming others, they became a social badge of honor. "Rather than exclude individuals from the group," Terrion explained, "putdowns seemed to include them by signaling that they were important enough to notice and were respected enough to withstand the insult, thus fostering a sense of acceptance and belongingness." The most effective jabs, and the ones that drew the most laughter, "were those that targeted popular and well-respected group members. It is precisely because the members enjoyed high status that they were 'safe' targets to laugh at."

The reason that edgy humor has received such a bad rap in the psychological community is its apparent similarity to bullying. But whereas bullying uses humor to shame and insult a member of a group, friendly put-downs serve the opposite function. There are two reasons why edgy humor surfaces in a group setting. The first has to do with group cohesion. As Terrion explained, "Put-downs reaffirm and reinforce camaraderie." You have to feel comfortable and secure enough with the other people in order to be able to tease them. "Mutual putdowns implicitly symbolize that 'We are close enough that we can say anything about each other.'" There's a certain degree of familiarity that allows members of a group to be informal and casually blunt with one another.

The other function that put-downs serve is to diffuse tension through the creation of mock conflict. As one of the officers explained to Terrion, "If we can't laugh at ourselves, or allow other people to laugh at us at times . . . then we're taking this world too seriously." Take Officer MJ's mocking disparagement of LJ's presentation. There is nothing inherently amusing about the incident except when it's placed in the underlying context of professionals who are tacitly competing with one another in the same field. Put-downs introduce a colloquial quality to group dynamics; they encourage a more relaxed, looser style of interaction. This helps to channel the tension of competitiveness, stress, fear, and unfamiliarity by turning it into a playful interaction.

Despite the important social function that aggressive humor serves, it is not always successful. In order for bantering to work, the other person needs to appreciate it as a tacit compliment. If the subject of the joke or barb is offended, humor's beneficial effects are seriously undermined. A notable negative incident took place when one of the officers targeted DS, the only female officer in the group. At the end of the third week, the instructor announced that any participants who were going to drive home for the weekend could leave a bit early. Thirteen people stood up, eliciting laughter. When the woman officer headed for the door, MJ—the officer who had sarcastically complimented LJ's presentation—called her out: "Oh, DS, you changed your mind, you decided to go, eh?" The group laughed, because it implied that DS was using the opportunity as an excuse to escape early from class. But DS was not amused. Caught off guard by the comment, she blushed and quickly left the classroom. She clearly felt that her actions were being criticized and experienced the event as a form of bullying. Later MJ apologized. "I'm sorry, I didn't mean to embarrass you, but I was beating you up like I would beat up one of the guys and how one of the other guys would beat me up."

Why was DS offended? Was the fact that she was the lone woman officer in the group a factor? Some researchers have observed that men are more prone to engage in put-downs than women. The male police officers seemed to intuitively realize that women did not think as highly of their humor as they did. Every time Terrion interviewed the men about their bantering, at least some of them claimed that *they* didn't find it funny, even though Terrion observed them laughing when the jabs took place. "'I don't know if I laughed at that one or not," said one male officer as he tried to reframe and hedge his recollection about a put-down that he and the rest of the class had found amusing. "I didn't get much out of that [joke]," another said. Many officers, in retrospect, found a number of instances of aggressive humor to be "offensive, embarrassing, or inappropriate." Some participants conveniently managed to forget about their humorous exchanges altogether. "I don't remember it."

Although Terrion did her best to remain nonjudgmental and open, her presence as a woman seemed to instill a sense of doubt and uncertainty in the men. Had they offended her? Was their humor going too far? Unfortunately, those dynamics were never openly discussed, even by Terrion. Perhaps MJ's unsuccessful effort to poke fun at DS served as evidence that playful aggressive humor was a male-bonding process more than it was an *officer*-bonding experience.

What is clear is that humor, when it's successful, has the power to relieve anxiety and bond people together. During times of adversity, when everything seems bleak, humor acts as a vital reminder that we don't have to remain stuck. We don't have to buy in to the heaviness and darkness of the situation. If we can find ways to laugh during such times, we can change perspective and view ourselves and our situation through a less drab and suffocating perspective. Coupled with an easy temperament, a sense of humor can help create an orientation to life that will protect us from the slings of hardship we're sure to encounter.

CONTACT

7

The Importance of a Satellite

Standing in front of a roomful of third graders, Pablo Pazmiño felt stumped. The twenty-one-year-old recent college graduate had never taught a class before or even taken a single education course. Now twenty-eight pairs of eyes were staring at him in anticipation. Pazmiño quickly realized he was in over his head. "It's my first day teaching," he remembers, "and I don't know what the heck I'm doing. I didn't even know how to arrange the desks."

Pazmiño had gotten himself into this bind quite unexpectedly. Only a few months earlier he had been finishing up his premed studies at UCLA, "but because I started out in engineering," he explains, "I hadn't yet completed all my biology requirements." Without all the necessary coursework under his belt, Pazmiño had to sit out a medical school admission cycle. He considered accepting a job at a doctor's office or working in a research lab, but neither option truly appealed to him. Pazmiño's parents even invited him to move back home. Then he happily stumbled across a teaching position on one of UCLA's job boards.

Landing a job as a public school teacher without a background in education is practically unheard of today, but in the mid-1990s California was in the throes of a booming economy unlike anything it had witnessed before. The state was sitting on a huge revenue windfall—which in retrospect it should have saved for a rainy day—and no one knew exactly what to do with the surplus. Eventually, some of the money was earmarked for education, but it came with a catch: in order for schools to qualify for the extra funding, they needed to significantly reduce their class size. That meant that public schools desperately needed teachers—and fast. The only state requirement that new college graduate recruits needed to fulfill was to pass the California Basic Educational Skills Test, a standardized exam covering basic reading and math skills. Fortunately for Pazmiño, he had just taken the Medical College Admission Test (MCAT). The skills test, in comparison, was a breeze.

"So I went to L.A. Unified with my test scores," Pazmiño recalls, "and they saw that I only missed two questions on the entire test. They basically told me I could teach anything I wanted." With all options open to him, Pazmiño could have decided to teach biology, chemistry, or even calculus. But instead he asked for a third-grade class in a struggling elementary school.

The reason for Pazmiño's selection has to do more with his own educational history than with anything else. If you ask any group of aspiring doctors to reflect on their early schooling, you're likely to hear plenty of stories about receiving straight As and being a teacher's pet. But for reasons that are still not completely clear to him, when Pazmiño was growing up, his teachers continuously pegged him as a mediocre student. "It would drive me nuts," Pazmiño recalls, "because whatever I turned in, it'd always come back as a B—even when I was turning in truly quality stuff."

Pazmiño didn't let this get in his way, but he always wondered in the back of his mind how it had affected him. What power do teachers hold? What if his instructors had rooted for him instead of just tolerated him? How would his experience have been different?

Now Pazmiño had a chance to approach it from the other side, coming at education from the role of a teacher. He decided to carry out a social experiment of sorts. What would happen, he wondered, if he became the sort of teacher he had always wanted to have when he was younger? Could he make a measurable difference in students' lives?

On his first day at Grant Elementary, a subperforming public school in Hollywood, Pazmiño was excited about the challenge. But what he hadn't taken into account was how the new, smaller classes would be created. In order to reduce the student-teacher ratio, all the third-grade teachers had been asked to transfer seven of their own students to Pazmiño's class. "So let me ask you," Pazmiño says. "Do you think the teachers took out their seven favorites? No, they selected their seven most troubled kids from each classroom—the ones who had disciplinary problems, the ones who were dragging their classroom behind, the ones who could barely speak any English. You name it, I got it. They put them in my class until they had twenty-eight."

Pazmiño had wanted a challenge, but this group of students was more than what he bargained for. "I heard *nightmare* stories about these kids, how crazy and out of control they were." It didn't help that on the morning of his first day, before the students arrived, the principal came by to wish him luck and forewarn him about his class. "This is such a dire situation," she confessed, "that all I hope is that somehow you teach them the multiplication table before the school year is over. Don't worry about anything else. If you can get them to that level, then at least they won't be too much behind in math for the fourth grade."

With his original lesson plans now scrapped, Pazmiño had to quickly come up with another strategy. When the bell rang and students streamed into the classroom, he remained quiet. Instead of proceeding with the usual introductions and first-day activities, the rookie teacher took a seat behind his table. "I just sat down, and I didn't say anything to the class for two days. They would just sit there. And I would just write at my desk. I was writing letters. And any time anybody started making noise, I'd look up and give them that lifted-eyebrow look. And they instantly shut up. I was like, 'Hmm, hmm,' and I'd get back to writing. They said, 'But, Mr. Pazmiño—' and I'd look at them. That kept them in line, and I refused to talk to them for two days."

Pazmiño adopted this unusual strategy not just to set the tone of the class. He used the time to write personalized letters to the parents of each student. "The letters were all a variation on the same theme," he explains. "'Dear Ms. Ochoa, Fernando is not allowed to play video games or watch TV until he learns his multiplication tables.'" Pazmiño figured that he could use all the help he could get from home. "My theory was, let me teach them multiplication and division during the first couple of months, and then I'll have the rest of the year to do what I actually want." On the third day, Pazmiño got down to business. He devoted the entire class time—and every subsequent day—to getting every student on board. He broke down the math for them, drilled them on multiplication problems, and tested them until he got the results he wanted. "At the end of the first month," Pazmiño proudly recalls, "wouldn't you know it, all these kids knew their multiplication tables, front and back."

But more important, Pazmiño earned their respect. And they were now on a par—at least mathematically—with the rest of their peers.

Up until now in our investigation of tunnelers, we have focused on the internal dynamics that come into play when individuals overcome adversity—on the inner drive and the orientation that protects tunnelers from the effects of adversity. But what about our interactions with the people around us? How do the individuals in our lives influence our ability to overcome adversity? Why is it that being around people like, say, Pazmiño can bring out the best in us?

Think back to any significant challenge you had to overcome in your life. Chances are you can point to a specific individual who was there to support you, whether a mentor, a good friend, or a trusted family member. He or she acts as a *satellite*—someone who is consistently available when needed, who's there as a point of strength. Studies that have tracked tunnelers have found that the presence of a supportive satellite figure is one of the differentiating variables that separate those who overcome life's obstacles from those who succumb to them. Knowing that we have someone on our side, someone to whom we can turn whenever we need help, makes enduring life's burdens a lot easier. As with the other tunneling qualities we've looked at, the importance of a satellite figure doesn't diminish as we become successful. Satellites continue to influence us throughout our lives.

Ellen A. Fagenson, who was affiliated with George Mason University, devoted her career to studying the role of satellites in the workplace. In what specific ways, she wondered, does a supportive person contribute to our career growth? When we think about work, we usually consider our short-term job-related tasks and long-term career prospects. We don't spend much time thinking about whether there's someone at the company who's truly looking out for us, someone we can trust unconditionally.

Fagenson mailed hundreds of surveys to random employees of a large international corporation, raising this very issue. Is there "someone in a position of power who looks out for you?" she inquired. Such a satellite figure, she clarified, might, among other things, share helpful advice or "bring your accomplishments to the attention of other people who have power in the company." About a third of the respondents—some from upper management, others from lower corporate tiers—were able to identify at least one person in the company who filled a satellite role. When she compared the employees who had identified a satellite at work with those who had not, she found that the individuals who had a satellite reported greater satisfaction at work, received more recognition from all of their supervisors, and were more likely to be promoted. This was true across the board for all employees who had someone there for them, regardless of gender or career position within the company. That is, whether you're just starting out or you're a senior manager, having a supportive figure in your life helps to shape your career.

What qualities, then, define a satellite? One of the most important ingredients is *unconditional positive regard,* a term coined by the psychologist Carl Rogers. It refers to the giving of support and acceptance with no strings attached—with no quid pro quo. A strong satellite is there no matter what, without an overriding agenda to govern the interaction.

It's a quality that Irvin Westheimer, a Cincinnati businessman, came to embody when he happened across a young boy scavenging for food near a trash pile in 1903. Westheimer felt so bad for the child that he approached him and offered to buy him a meal. The businessman later learned that the boy's dad had recently passed away and the family was struggling financially. Westheimer befriended the family and became a mentor to the young boy. Realizing that there were many other children who could benefit from this type of mentoring relationship, he recruited colleagues and friends to form an organization that paired youngsters in need with caring satellite figures.

Around the same time that Westheimer organized his group of volunteers, a New York City court clerk named Ernest Coulter felt heartbroken by the thousands of indigent children he saw passing through the court system on a regular basis. Most of the youngsters, Coulter believed, were not criminals at heart but rather children who did not have anyone in their lives to direct them. There was a better way to help them, he figured. Like

Westheimer in Cincinnati, Coulter in New York organized a group of volunteers, urging them to "make the little chap feel that there is at least one human being in this great city who takes a personal interest in him, who cares whether he live or dies."

Eventually the independent grassroots efforts in the two cities merged to form the Big Brothers Big Sisters (BBBS) organization. Today BBBS brings together prescreened adult volunteers with children who are in desperate need of a satellite. But what does it mean to be a big brother or big sister? Do the mentors tutor academically, teach social skills, or engage in conflict resolution? The unique and fascinating thing about BBBS is that there is no prescribed agenda for the interaction between child and adult. The volunteers are not there to help the children with their schoolwork, impart life skills, or help them out in any other specific way per se. The only requirement for the volunteers is that they meet with their assigned child at least twice a month, for roughly three to four hours per visit. The point is for the kids to spend quality time the way they would with, well, an older brother or sister. They can sit and talk, attend sporting events, watch a movie, or just hang out.

Do these interactions really make a difference? Can being there for someone unconditionally—in and of itself—make a substantial contribution? Jean Baldwin Grossman, a professor of public and international affairs at Princeton University, asked herself this exact question. She decided to perform an evaluation to determine whether the BBBS has any measurable, concrete beneficial effects on children's lives. After all, how much of a difference can spending a few hours with a child really make? Obviously, for a young person, it must be nice to have an adult satellite with whom you can kick back every other week, but can those limited, agenda-free interactions affect the more serious underlying problems and issues in the child's life?

To find out, Grossman teamed up with an associate and collected data on hundreds of BBBS children from all across the country. She compared the children who were matched with a BBBS volunteer with those kids who were on a wait list because not enough big brothers and sisters are available (BBBS is always looking for dedicated volunteers and is especially short on men). From a scientific perspective, the wait-list kids acted as the perfect control group, because the children who were paired with a big brother or a big sister were selected randomly. The benefit of a random design is that it eliminates any variables that might otherwise skew the results.

A year and a half into their survey, Grossman compared those children who were assigned a big brother or sister with those who remained on the wait list. She found that the BBBS experience made an incredible difference. BBBS kids were 45.8 percent less likely to use drugs than their counterparts. They were also 32 percent less likely to engage in a violent fight, they skipped school 52 percent fewer days, and they reported lying to their parents 37 percent less often than the wait-list children. These differences are remarkable when you consider that the volunteers were not trained to address school, friendship, or family issues. All the big brothers and big sisters did was to be there unconditionally for their assigned child. But knowing that there is somebody out there who cares for you, someone whom you can talk to about anything, someone who's not going to judge you, means the world to a kid whose entire world might be falling apart. The satellite's unconditional positive regard permeates to other areas of life. Like the office workers who reported greater overall career success when they knew someone was there for them, at-risk children improved their overall behavior when they knew that they had a supportive satellite figure.

The unconditional quality of satellites is so important that it can even transform the lives of those who have to endure the most tragic events. In 1945 Jewish organizations persuaded the British government to allow a limited number of children refugees who lived in Nazi-occupied territories into the country. These children had become separated from their parents and families during the war and were living as orphans. Some of the kids had spent the war years in hiding; others had survived the concentration camps. Great Britain reluctantly agreed to open its doors to the young refugees as long as the Jewish organizations agreed to assume the financial obligation of the project: flying the children into the country, finding them a place to live, and feeding and clothing them. That was no easy task for the Jewish community, given that the economy was in shambles.

Alice Goldberger, a German refugee herself, accepted the challenge of caring for a large group of these children. With a shoestring budget that was barely sufficient for food, Goldberger happily accepted a donation by a generous benefactor who would let her and her children stay in a large home in the country. There was no budget, however, for new clothes or new toys. Everything they got came from hand-me-down donations. And if a child needed anything that could not be found in the donation pile, Goldberger herself had to plead for it in front of the Central British Fund for Jewish Relief.

A house in the country is certainly a nice place to live in, but there was a limit to how many children it could hold. In May 1946 the home was virtually filled to capacity when Goldberger received a phone call asking how many empty beds she had available. Not wanting to turn any child away, Goldberger figured she could possibly accommodate two more youngsters, four at most. There was a pause on the other end of the line, followed by an apologetic admission from the caller, who told Goldberger that he had just sent eleven children, all survivors of Auschwitz, to her country house.

The physical and monetary constraints, as inconvenient as they were, were not the chief problem for Goldberger and her two assistants. The children had witnessed unspeakable events with which they could not cope psychologically. One young child constantly asked the adults around him whether they were aware that his parents had been shot. Another young girl couldn't forgive her mother for being taken away from her. "She came into the room, gave me a piece of bread, and said she would come back soon, but she never came." Some of the children were so traumatized that they questioned whether Goldberger and the country home were just another Nazi ruse.

Amid all of the turmoil, Goldberger remained a beacon of support. When the children under her care experienced night terrors, for example, Goldberger soothed them by playing the harmonica until they fell back to sleep. "Alice was really there for us, night or day," remembers one of the women who stayed with Goldberger as a little girl. "She was never 'off.' I think that's what home is. She never criticized you. And she understood everything."

The psychological and emotional impact of the children's trauma could rise suddenly and unexpectedly. "I had taken the children for a walk in the woods," remembered Goldberger, "and I was walking along, holding some by the hand, singing." Suddenly she was knocked to the ground as the children huddled next to her, screaming in panic. When she finally managed to calm the youngsters, Goldberger realized that they had reacted to the faint sounds of a barking dog in the distance. "They were frightened to death of dogs," she explained, "because the Nazis used dogs to frighten the captives. Every dog was a threat. The fear persisted for some children for a long time." Two years after the war had ended, Goldberger took the children to London for a field trip. Some children still feared that the buses would transport them to a concentration camp.

Goldberger's children had gone through so much and needed so much attention that Goldberger always felt that she was playing catch-up. But the one principle that she honored above everything else was to accept and support the children without fail and without judgment. "Alice had a talent for finding something you were good at and helping you grow into it," one of Goldberger's boys remembered decades later. "She knew I was crazy about planes and arranged for me to meet with a real pilot several times." When an eight-year-old girl insisted on wearing the cross that had been given to her by nuns who had taken care of her during the war, Goldberger didn't flinch. Here was a child who appeared to surrender her Jewish identity. But Goldberger believed that the young girl's autonomy and personal dignity were more important than the symbolic implication of what it meant for a Jewish Holocaust survivor to be wearing a cross.

Remarkably, the vast majority of the orphaned refugees grew up to lead normal, successful lives. Many of them credited Goldberger with their success in adulthood. "Up until my midtwenties," recalled a former boy resident, "perhaps I did feel that if things were really bad, that there was someone you could turn to without having to swallow your pride. . . . So in that sense she might have been like a mother." The children adored Goldberger because of her unconditional acceptance of them and her consistent presence in their lives.

Goldberger's work with the children was obviously much more intense and demanding than the work a BBBS volunteer performs, but there's an underlying similarity. In both cases the element of unconditional support plays an integral role in the function of a satellite or mentor. For both parents and managers, it's easy to overlook how important that unconditional support can be. We're so used to paying attention to the other details of leadership—whether setting boundaries, providing feedback, or teaching—that we sometimes forget to communicate the most basic element: that we're there to be counted on no matter what.

Robin Pollock, a vocational researcher, interviewed dozens of middle- and upper-level managers in various industries, from agriculture to finance, and asked them about their interaction with their mentors at work. Pollock was surprised to learn that the survey participants reported receiving little concrete help from their most important support people. The strength of the relationship didn't emanate from receiving career advice, on-the-job training, or coaching in company politics; it was the quality of the relationship itself that benefited the employees.

What makes mentors most effective, Pollock discovered, is their ability to balance being respectful with challenging those they are supporting. Finding that equilibrium is not always easy. Though it's certainly important to be supportive and encouraging, if that's all a satellite does, he or she risks coming across as less a wise mentor and more like Barney the Dinosaur. Mentors who offer only compliments—"Super dee duper! I'm so proud of you!"—are in danger of being viewed as fake and empty.

That's where "tough" skills come in handy. Mentors who are not afraid to challenge—question, dare, disagree—can make a huge difference in the lives of those they mentor. And they come across more authentically because they are not overly saccharine. But offering a challenging comment works only when there's already an underlying foundation of respect. There also needs to be a clear and unambiguous understanding that the relationship is based on unconditional positive support. Otherwise the words of advice can be perceived as an unwelcome, even tyrannical, critique. The key is to be honest and direct while also being caring and respectful. That's what makes it so challenging. When we're in a position of power, most of us either think of ourselves as the "authority figure" who lays down the law or the "nice guy/gal" who's there to be a friend and supporter. Combining the two—which is what makes for an ideal mentor—forces us to consistently shift roles. It's a delicate balancing act for which, it turned out, third-grade teacher Pablo Pazmiño had a special knack.

The reason Pazmiño was able to get through to his kids—remember, they were considered the worst in their cohort—is that he challenged them to go to the next level while letting them know that he cared about them, that he was proud of them, and that he was there for them every step of the way. When Pazmiño saw a child who was lagging behind, instead of embarrassing him in front of the class or giving up on him, he looked for an excuse to spend more one-on-one time with the student. He did so without the child or anyone else in the class realizing that there was an academic issue. "I had this policy," Pazmiño explains, "that if someone misbehaved, they'd get 'benched,' which meant that they had to sit out recess. So for students who needed extra help, I would find ways throughout the day to bench them. That way they had to stay with me and spend extra time learning. If Fernando needed extra help, I might see him looking out the window, and I'd go, 'Hey, Fernando, welcome to bench.'" None of the children enjoyed being benched, of course, but Pazmiño realized that it was the easiest way of helping them without shaming them or singling them out. Whenever a student complained about having to miss recess, Pazmiño would commiserate, "Hey, I'm losing my lunch hour too, Buddy."

Four months into the school year, Pazmiño asked the other teachers what they did when they completed the math workbook. "Mr. Pazmiño, I've been here for twenty-five years," one of the senior teachers informed him, "and we've never finished the math workbook." Pazmiño thanked him politely. "Of course, in my head I was thinking 'We completed the workbook last week.'"

Pazmiño had instinctively incorporated all of the best satellite attitudes. He challenged his students—who had behavioral problems and learning disabilities—to perform *above* their class level. He was there for them unconditionally whenever they needed help. And he let them know how much they meant to him. "I was handing out tests, and these kids were getting A, A, A. I was really proud of them."

But now Pazmiño ran into an unexpected problem. Having maxed out the math workbook for the year, what would he do now? He figured he was on his own. So he went to Barnes & Noble, bought a number of higher-grade-level math books, and made photocopies for his students. "I started teaching them pre-algebra. And then I started teaching them algebra."

Pazmiño had decided to be a teacher in the first place because he wanted to treat his students the way he had wanted to be treated by his teachers when he was younger. On the one hand, he demanded and expected more of his students than anyone else ever had. But at the same time, he talked to them the way he did to his friends, something not many instructors feel comfortable enough to do. When the class performed especially well on a test, he handed out the exams and quoted a lyric from a Blackstreet song, "Hey, I like the way you worked this." Without missing a beat, one of his students sang out the next line, "No diggitty." Pazmiño saw it as one of the signs that he had genuinely bonded with his students. "It was funny that he knew the song," Pazmiño reflects, "and that he knew I knew that song." The young teacher interwove pop culture references into his lessons, made up his own terminology when necessary, and used slang without thinking twice about it. In his role as teacher, Pazmiño was the students' best friend and their harshest critic rolled into one.

Once Pazmiño could see that his students were excelling in math, he branched out to other subjects. He worked with them on their reading skills, eventually assigning them *Charlotte's Web* (a fifth-grade reading-level book). He then covered anatomy for good measure. "I was like, 'If I had to study this as a premed student, then you guys have to study it, too.'" He refused to dumb it down. "It wasn't 'The hand bone is connected to the wrist bone.' It was all about the hypoglottis and trachea and femur. And these are the same children who couldn't even speak English properly at the beginning of the year."

Pazmiño was having so much fun teaching that he decided to postpone his medical school studies another year and stay with his class through fourth grade. His efforts during his first year of teaching did not go unnoticed. For his accomplishments, the Los Angeles school district honored him with the "Rookie of the Year" teaching award. And the next year Pazmiño picked up where he had left off. "By the end of my second year teaching, we stopped just short of analytical geometry. And they were getting As on their tests. Maybe one or two kids were getting a C. But still they were doing trigonometry in fourth grade."

Pazmiño remembers one day when the principal walked by the classroom and saw the blackboard. "She was just beside herself. 'What are you teaching these kids???'"

A couple of months before the summer vacation, the assistant principal entered his classroom and informed Pazmiño of a schedule change. "'I just wanted to let you know'—she kind of pulled me aside—'that we decided to move the break period from nine thirty to ten thirty A.M.' I said, 'Okay,' and she said, 'Okay, thank you. Good-bye.'" It was only then that Pazmiño realized—after teaching in the school for almost two years—that he was supposed to be giving his class an extra break every day. "You mean I was supposed to give them lunch *and* recess *and* a break? These kids were lucky to make it to recess, we had so much to cram in."

Today Pazmiño works as a spinal surgeon in southern California. But he fondly remembers his two-year stint as a teacher. "They were some of my most memorable moments in life," he recalls.

Examining Pazmiño's success as a teacher, we can attribute some of it to his motivation, intelligence, work ethic, leadership skills, and dedication. But perhaps most important was his intuitive ability to know how to be an effective satellite figure, interweaving challenging expectations with genuine respect. His stance toward his students transformed their lives. "More than ten years later, I still receive letters from them. School was always easy for them; we accomplished a lot in those two years."

Neuropsychologists know that in the first three years of life kids are like sponges, soaking in any information we give them. Their neural pathways are growing rapidly, making new connections. As we age, the window of opportunity diminishes. But it never fully closes. The right satellite can awaken new potential and possibilities in our lives and help overcome gaps in achievement. It's inspiring to see the glass ceilings that get broken when the power of the satellite-tunneler relationship is at work.

8

Putting It All into Practice

When I was in seventh grade, I wasn't crazy about school, but I looked forward to going to history class. It wasn't because I cared so much about the subject—to my twelve-year-old mind, anything that happened before I was born seemed irrelevant—but my class was filled with so many characters that I felt like I was entering the set of a reality show. There was Tracey, who always looked stylish and hip and was fearless in the face of authority. And Carlos, who dressed in Mexican gangster attire—with the full regalia of khaki pants with an unbuttoned flannel shirt draped over a white undershirt—looked like he could pass for eighteen but never cared enough about school to pass a single test.

Our teacher, Mrs. Davenport, was the odd one out. She was one of the sweetest and kindest instructors I had ever had—not an obvious match for our class of motley characters. Mrs. Davenport had come out of retirement to return to teaching, as she continuously reminded us. "This is the worst class I have ever had in my twenty-five years of teaching," she'd lament half to herself and half to the class at large. "If I had known how bad it would be, I would've never come out of retirement."

I was well behaved back then, but our class as a whole had

a lot of attitude even for seventh graders, and Mrs. Davenport didn't quite know what to do with us.

To make matters worse, not all of us spoke English well. That was only my second year in the United States, and even though I could communicate well, my vocabulary wasn't strong. Mrs. Davenport sat all of the English as a Second Language (ESL) students in the same section of the classroom, because we were given a special textbook. Instead of the normal seventh-grade history book, our group was assigned a simplified version, with big fonts and lots of pictures. It looked as though it was meant for a third grader, but we loved it. It made learning a breeze. Nonetheless, despite the undemanding work, most of my ESL classmates, including Carlos, failed every test. It wasn't because their English wasn't strong enough or that they couldn't handle the material. They just never really tried.

But something changed dramatically in the spring of that year. It started when I received a quiz back with a grade of 84, lower than I had hoped for but still acceptable. Then I noticed that my friend sitting to my left had also gotten an 84. I was more surprised that he had passed the quiz than that we had received an identical score. I turned my head and saw that everyone around me had scored an 84—even Carlos. And in case I had any lingering doubts, I noticed that everyone had missed the same two questions I had missed. The moment they realized I had caught on to the fact that they had copied my quiz answers, they started laughing. They could see the look on my face as I put it all together. To be honest, I really didn't mind that they'd copied my answers. I took it as a compliment that they considered me smart enough to cheat off of. I was actually more surprised than anything else; it was the first time my ESL classmates had showed any evidence that they cared about grades.

I don't know why Mrs. Davenport didn't say anything about the cheating incident—it's hard to believe that she missed it, given how obvious it was. Maybe she was so overwhelmed with our class that she just stopped caring. Or maybe she just figured that the students were putting at least *some* effort into their schoolwork. Whatever her reason, she let everyone get away with it. And as it turned out, that was the best thing she could have done.

From that moment on, Carlos started caring. He handed in his homework, studied for his tests, and put in the effort. He was still the same Carlos, dressed in the same threads, wearing that chill and aloof facial expression. But he became one of the best students in the class. And as far as I know, he never cheated once after that incident—at least not off me.

And we never talked about it.

During the last week of school, Mrs. Davenport gave out special certificates to all the students who had received straight As in the class (there weren't many of us). Then she paused and, once more, referred to her twenty-five-year tenure as a teacher. But this time, instead of chastising us for being her least favorite class, she pointed to Carlos and said that she had never seen a student turn his grades around so dramatically. She invited him to come up to receive a certificate. Carlos walked to the front, with the same semidetached demeanor he always displayed, but you could tell that he took Mrs. Davenport's ceremony seriously, that he cared, and that he was touched by her gesture.

Carlos and I never once talked about studying or school or grades. I'm not sure exactly what caused Carlos to change. I'm not sure that he would have known either if someone had asked him. The initial cheating incident had probably started out as a joke, but when Carlos got the quiz back and saw he got a good grade it seemed to spark an interest in him. Or perhaps he figured that if one of his friends got good grades, why couldn't he? Regardless of how the transformation came about exactly, I seemed to play an unintentional role as a satellite. I made no effort to specifically influence Carlos, and possibly I had nothing at all to do with it. But on some level I believe I gave a signal to the others that I wasn't even aware of sending.

One of the things I've seen as a psychologist is that those moments when we touch someone else's life are more common than we realize. Think back in your own life to a comment that someone made to you that stayed with you and that you held on to for years. Or think of a time when someone thanked you for something you said to them long ago; you don't even remember saying it, but they really valued and remembered it.

What if we could make a more conscious effort to have a positive influence on people's lives? More specifically, what's the most effective way of putting into practice everything we've learned about what distinguishes tunnelers from the rest of us and used it to change and improve? In this chapter, I'll look at some practical ways we can empower and inspire those around us—our employees, our children, and, maybe most important, ourselves.

We can read about tunnelers' drive and orientation, and though it can make perfect sense, implementing those qualities in our own lives on a day-to-day basis is not always easy. Here are some ways of keeping these qualities in mind:

Yourself

1. *Shift the focus back to you*. Whenever you're facing a difficult situation, especially one where you feel that you were treated unfairly, ask yourself what it is that *you* can do to change the dynamics of the situation. Remember the importance of the limelight effect. Accept that the situation happened. Yes, other people play a part. Yes, there may have been circumstances out of your control. But now ask yourself what *you* can do about it. What actions can you take in the future? What changes can you make in terms of how you approached the situation? What can you learn from it? What can you do differently next time? It's easy and tempting to shift the blame or focus to others. But you achieve the most success when you put yourself in the driver's seat.

2. *Search out meaning*. Whenever you spot anything that's meaningful to you, even if it seems trivial or irrelevant, follow up on your interest. Learn more about it. Even if

the information ends up having no real practical purpose, that process of discovery alone can energize and infuse you with creativity and passion. It can stimulate other aspects of your life. Every so often—probably more frequently than we realize—something that started out as a hobby or casual pursuit ends up having a big impact on the direction of our lives.

3. *Stay calm.* Don't let the little things in life—the mistakes, regrets, annoyances—upset your day or your life. The sooner you can let all that go, the better you will be able to get where you want to go. If you find yourself caught in minutiae, take a step back; look at the bigger picture. Weeks or years down the road, you won't even remember what's so upsetting to you at the moment. Develop an easy temperament. When you do, you'll find that many of your problems will take care of themselves without your having to do much about them. Even when it comes to life's bigger problems, not obsessing about the details and holding on to all that we have going for us help put everything into perspective.

4. *Stay the course.* When we try something challenging and don't get the results that we want, we are tempted to give up. That's because it can feel overwhelming and disappointing. At least by quitting, we think, we can reclaim some of our power. But the fact is that there'll always be

difficult times and dark moments. If you decide to give up on something, make sure it's because the goal is no longer something you are interested in, not because you've hit a snag or obstacle in the process.

5. *Give yourself a break.* We're used to thinking of success in immediate terms. When we don't achieve our goals right away, or when we hit an obstacle, the negative self-script in our heads starts to run. We become critical, doubting ourselves and dismissing our efforts. There's a double standard in place. If we had a friend go through a similar difficult period, we'd likely be supportive and encouraging. We certainly wouldn't put him or her down. *Don't treat yourself any differently than you would your best friend.*

6. *Don't be afraid to use humor.* How often do you allow yourself to laugh about things that are going on in your life? And how often do you spend time laughing with those who are closest to you? Humor is a powerful tool to get through hard times. Use it liberally.

7. *Be on the lookout for satellites.* Whenever you come across someone who seems interested in you or who seems reliable, respectful, and willing to challenge you, capitalize on the opportunity. Let him or her know that you'd like to keep in touch. Invite him or her for coffee or lunch. Even if your contact with the person is sporadic or done via

e-mail, do your best to maintain a relationship. Call on that person when you're at an important crossroad or facing challenging times.

8. *Allow yourself to become inspired.* Looking at all the different stories of tunnelers discussed in this book, which ones do you find most touching? If you look at your own life, what are your favorite tunneling moments? What are some of the memorable times when you had to fight to make it, when you persevered and achieved success when you weren't "supposed to"? Look at your life for tunneling experiences of your own. Use them to inspire future success. Too often we take our own experiences in overcoming adversity for granted.

Employees

As we've seen, the same qualities that help young people overcome adversity help the rest of us excel in life. When you're an employer or manager, you have the opportunity to help others reach new career and personal heights that they might not have even aspired to. Here are some of the ways to instill tunneling attributes in those who work for us.

1. *Seek their input.* Sometimes we neglect to ask for opinions and input from those who work for us because we fear coming across as incompetent (e.g., "I don't know what

I'm doing") or we're afraid we'll get an answer we don't like and then we'll be stuck with it. Inviting subordinates to participate in the decision-making process, however, gives them a voice and empowers them. Instead of simply being cogs in the machine, they are taken seriously. It is a great way to shift their limelight so that they realize they can effect change in both the company and their careers.

2. *Add fuel to the fire.* When you notice that employees are passionate about a project, a topic, or anything else, jump on it. Assign them a leadership role in that capacity. They'll get more meaning out of their job and recognize that you value their passion if you encourage them to be creative and explore new roles. Imagine what it would feel like if a manager always noticed when you felt energized about something and then opened the door for you to immerse yourself in that new area.

3. *Act like a hall of fame coach.* Any good coach whose team has fallen behind will encourage his or her players to step up, give it their best effort, and not give up on the game. During difficult times, employees sometimes lose momentum and start second-guessing their actions. Remind them of the good things that they've done and how much you appreciate their dedication. These are more than just pep talks; it shows them that you are relentless in pursu-

ing goals and that things are continuing to move forward despite the current setbacks.

4. *Model.* During times of stress your employees will look at you to see how you're coping. If you're calm and collected while remaining sharp and engaged, those around you will adopt your attitude. Use humor to deflate intense situations; it shows that no matter how difficult things become, you are able to stay unaffected.

5. *Think of your employees as family.* Take an interest in your employees the way you do with your family members. When you do, you'll be communicating respect and high regard. If you feel a strong connection with some of them or particular pride in their work, let them know. If you feel concerned about how they are doing, communicate that. When your employees know you value them, they'll recognize that you are truly there for them. Try to act as a mentor to all of them. If some of them are more difficult, try to see what is standing in the way and work to change it.

6. *Show them that they're better than they realize.* Do you see strengths in others that they can't fully see in themselves? Tell them. Encourage them to develop those hidden gifts. Give them a project or assignment that will force them to utilize those strengths. They might at first feel challenged

or even overwhelmed, but they'll appreciate your belief in them and will ultimately come to see and appreciate those qualities in themselves.

7. *Share.* If you notice a quality in an employee that's especially unique or appealing, tell him or her. Your words and opinions are more important to your employees than you realize. We often assume that people see themselves the same way we see them. But that's usually not the case. And even if your opinion doesn't come across as news to your employees, it's always good for them to know that their supervisor is aware of their ability as well.

Children

With all the parenting philosophies out there, it seems as though every year something else is in vogue. And most of it seems to be based on opinion. Whatever your individual parenting style, try to incorporate a few of these research-backed suggestions:

1. *Give your children choices.* Sure, left completely to their own devices, most kids would spend all their money on chocolate and ice cream or watch TV 24/7. There's a reason that parents need to be actively involved in their children's lives. But though kids don't always make the right decisions, allow them to make as many as possible within accepted boundaries. The more control they feel they have

over their lives, the more they'll develop an inner locus of control. When children realize that they have control over their environment, they take responsibility for themselves.

Parents sometimes view offering their children choices as a waste of time. Why ask a child which pair of socks he or she would like to wear? Children take more ownership of what goes on around them when they're asked to be involved. Parents often don't realize how many opportunities are out there to make choices: Which song would you like to listen to? Which vegetable would you like to eat first? Do you want to talk about this now or later? Which area of your room would you like to start cleaning up? Whom would you like to play with today? It's important that the choices be genuine choices, not forced ones or veiled threats. ("Do you want to clean up your room, or do you want me to get really angry?" doesn't count as a choice.)

2. *Follow the meaning.* What interests your child? Whether it's dinosaurs, sketching, singing, soccer, or baseball, find out what your children love to do and help engage them in that activity. If they develop a special interest in, say, astronomy, nurture that interest. Immerse yourself in astronomy as well. Look up information with them online, or read a book together. Search for planetarium events and surprise them with a visit. Buy an inexpensive telescope to look at the night sky together. Come up with

fun astronomical projects that you can do together. If you teach your children to pursue what's interesting or meaningful to them, they'll be able to more easily develop an appreciation for meaning later on. In addition, pursuing something they're already interested in will help them expand their horizons and build a stronger bond with you as you explore it together. And if you really want to wow your child, plan a surprise day around his or her interest, putting together one activity after another that share the same theme.

3. *Know when to quit and when to persevere.* If your child wants to quit a hobby, class, or project, ask yourself, is it because of a temporary setback, or is there a good underlying reason? Talk it through. Break it down together. Sometimes a child might feel he has taken on too much or has lost interest in a hobby or sport, in which case it might make sense to quit. But if there's an obstacle that came up, perhaps there is a way for him to overcome it. Can you solve it together? Encourage your child to try to resolve the problem, and delay the decision to quit. If, after addressing the problem, he still wants to quit, you can say how proud you are that he gave it his best effort. And if he overcame the obstacle and decided to remain involved, that makes for an even more interesting discussion about not allowing hardships to derail you from something that you care about.

4. *Model an easygoing temperament.* Your children have no
control over their temperament. They might be born
easygoing, or they might have a finicky disposition. But
you have control over the way you come across to them. If
you can remain calm and collected, your children will start
picking up on these qualities. The temperament they're
born with is shaped by the environment in which they
grow. And if they see that you don't make a big fuss about
little things and don't get overwhelmed by unexpected
obstacles, they'll start adopting the same attitude. One
of the biggest mistakes parents make is adopting a perfectionist outlook. If mistakes are not tolerated, children
can become anxious and see themselves as not being good
enough. They can internalize elements of the perfectionist attitude and come to view themselves as deficient. This
can lead to a lack of confidence and an inability to value
themselves properly. A perfectionist attitude can also lead
to eating disorders (aiming for the "perfect" weight) and
lying or developing a tendency to harbor secrets (if something is short of perfect, I can't share it).

5. *Laugh about things.* Do you and your children share inside jokes? Do you act silly together? Can you laugh off
mistakes instead of overly intellectualizing them? Humor
strengthens the bonds between parents and children. And
a healthy sense of humor is associated with higher intelligence. It might feel as though you're goofing off, but

your children get a lot more from funny family moments than meets the eye. Plus, having a laugh together makes parenting a lot more fun.

6. *Communicate love and respect.* It's easy to assume that children know that their parents love and respect them. But when parents take that knowledge for granted and forget to tell them explicitly, children may assume that their parents do not care. As a psychologist I often talk with parents who are worried and concerned about their children. I find that many parents focus so much time and energy on fixing the problems that they forget to tell their children how much they mean to them, how proud of them they are, and how they feel about them. Some fear that coming across as too loving or respectful will lull a child into laziness. But the opposite is true. I find that children rise up to a challenge much more quickly if they feel they have a foundation of respect.

7. *Encourage them to take on challenges and stretch themselves.* Like most of us, children tend to underestimate their potential. Find an activity that's challenging and a bit out of their comfort range, and tackle it together. Whether it's going on a long hike or tackling an extra-credit science project, your child will experience how great it feels when he or she conquers something that seems impossibly difficult. Especially when you incorporate humor, respect, and

an easygoing temperament, it sends a message that the challenges they face in life needn't feel suffocating; they can be exciting and rewarding.

8. *Let them know you're always there for them.* The unconditional positive regard aspect of a satellite is an element most people tend to take for granted. Letting your children know that you're always there for them, no matter what, is very reassuring; convey your love and respect for them. Although most parents do this instinctively, they often don't think to regularly communicate their feelings to their children. For children, it's one thing to have a sense that their parents care about them abstractly, another thing to hear it reinforced throughout their lives.

9. *Let them know you're part of a team.* Let your children know that whatever they're going through, you are on their side—that you're all part of the same team. It is especially important for them to remember this when there are disagreements or angry words exchanged. None of this should change the fact that you're operating as a family unit.

10. *Treat them as you would your best friends.* There's a common adage in parenting classes that you shouldn't be friends with your children, that you need to be their parents first. And it's true that setting boundaries for

your kids is important. You can't hang out with them the way you would with a friend. But if you look at most of the suggestions listed above, they sound surprisingly like how you would treat your best friend—with respect and admiration, by being straight and honest with them, supportive, critical when necessary, but always unconditionally loyal.

Tunneling is such an important skill, you'd think we'd learn about it in school or in seminars at work. But fortunately, we have the research available to us; we can teach ourselves how to confront and overcome adversity. The other piece of good news is that the changes we need to embrace are relatively straightforward and completely within our control. *Remembering* to follow through in tough times when everything seems dire and hopeless is the only thing that's truly challenging.

Epilogue

When I was assigned a textbook chapter as a student, I'd laboriously make my way through the text with highlighter in hand. After reading the first few pages I'd flip to the end of the chapter to count the number of pages I had left. I wasn't averse to learning, but I've never liked textbooks. I find them dry and uninspiring. They take the juice out of learning.

For a long time I thought this view was universal. After all, how many people do you see reading textbooks on the beach for fun? How many textbooks have you read since you finished school?

When I taught psychology courses in graduate school, I decided to once and for all divorce myself from textbooks. I didn't want to inflict the same experience on my students that I had to endure. I assigned works by the original authors and included research articles that I found relevant and interesting.

Many of my students breathed a sigh of relief when they found out my class was going to be textbook free. But there were some students who approached me after class to ask whether I had a textbook to recommend. The request surprised me; but in retrospect I realized these students wanted a textbook because it suited their learning style. They actually appreciated the formal presentation of a textbook. They like to see the facts and figures laid out on the page.

I still am not partial to textbooks. I consciously wrote this book in a conversational, narrative way. But I recognize that the one problem with a more narrative writing style is that it can make it harder for readers to keep track of the underlying information. So what follows is a summary of the key points that I've covered in the book, for those who want to refresh themselves on the salient points.

First, remember that tunnelers are not superhuman. It's not as if they were born with some special spiritual or psychological gifts that they can draw on to carry them through life's struggles. They are just like you and me. But they routinely approach their lives from a slightly different perspective or angle. And that approach makes all the difference.

When tunnelers find themselves in difficult situations, they first look to themselves to see what they can do to change the situation. They don't waste time pointing the fingers at external circumstances, or at others. Rather, they take responsibility for their lives and hold themselves accountable first and foremost for what happens. Even when others around them succumb to hardships or difficult circumstances, tunnelers refuse to let go of their focus on themselves and what they can do to extricate themselves from the situation they find themselves in.

Because tunnelers focus on themselves as agents of responsibility, they seek out situations and interactions that are meaningful to them. If they can turn their calling in life into a career or profession, that's ideal. But their efforts aren't limited to that. Tunnelers look to squeeze meaning out of life wherever they can find it, and devote time to activities that offer them a sense of purpose. And when life itself does not feel very meaningful, they derive meaning from their search for meaning.

Once they discover that meaning, tunnelers hold on and don't let go. They are relentless in their pursuit of what they love. They refuse to give up just because they hit a wall. Or several walls. When they experience failure they don't lash out at others, or at the world. Instead, they push themselves to come up with a different way of making things work.

These three qualities—an internal focus, their quest for meaning, and their relentless pursuit—make up the inner drive that tunnelers rely on to overcome adversity. And they tend to do so while maintaining an even temperament and orientation. Instead of getting worked up or upset over bumps and irritations—instead of focusing on what's gone wrong—they tend to take a more relaxed attitude toward life. They don't let the small things get to them. After all, the way in which we react to small irritations in life helps to shape the way we react to the bigger events.

In addition, tunnelers tend to rely on humor in stressful situations to release tension, rather than becoming more intense and serious. They recognize humor for its ability to strengthen interpersonal connections.

And finally, when tunnelers meet someone who supports them unconditionally and who treats them with respect while continuing to challenge them, they hold on to and nurture their connection with that person.

I believe that by embracing these principles, all of us can learn how to better face and overcome adversity in our lives. Instead of giving in to events—no matter how challenging or difficult they may be—we can find ways to work through that adversity and appreciate life and its endless potential to the fullest. By following these principles, rather than becoming the victim of events, we can truly become the captains of our souls.

Notes

Chapter 1: Tunneling

Emmy Werner's longitudinal research of the Kauai cohort is presented in Emmy E. Werner and Ruth S. Smith, *Overcoming the Odds: High Risk Children from Birth to Adulthood* (Ithaca, N.Y.: Cornell University Press, 1992). To learn more about other longitudinal studies, see Emmy Werner, "What Can We Learn About Resilience from Large-Scale Longitudinal Studies?" in *Handbook of Resilience in Children,* ed. Sam Goldstein and Robert B. Brooks (New York: Kluwer Academic/Plenum Publishers, 2005), pp. 91–105.

Norman Garmezy studied children born to schizophrenic parents and found that not all of them developed psychological maladies. See Garmezy, "Competence and Adaptation in Adult Schizophrenic Patients and Children at Risk," in *Schizophrenia: The First Ten Dean Award Lectures,* ed. Stanley R. Dean (New York: MSS Information Corp., 1973), pp. 163–204. A few years later, Michael Rutter published "Protective Factors in Children's Responses to Stress and Disadvantage" in *Annals Academy of Medicine Singapore* 8 (1979): 324–338.

You can read more about the Copenhagen schizophrenia study in "The Schizophrenia High-Risk Project in Copenhagen: Three Decades of Progress" by Tyrone Cannon and Sarnoff A. Mednick. It was published in *Acta Psychiatrica Scandinavica* 87 (1993): 33–47.

The New Zealand study that tracked a group of children over the span of twenty-one years is David M. Fergusson and L. John Horwood, "Resilience to Childhood Adversity: Results of a 21 Year Study," in *Resilience and Vulnerability: Adaptation in the Context of Childhood Adversities,* ed. Suniya S. Luthar (Cambridge, England: Cambridge University Press, 2003), pp. 130–155.

Kerry E. Bolger and Charlotte J. Patterson observed children who endured child abuse and their struggles with adversity. See Bolger and Patterson, "Sequelae of Child Maltreatment: Vulnerability and Resilience," in *Resilience and Vulnerability: Adaptation in the Context of Childhood Adversities,* ed. Suniya S. Luthar (Cambridge, England: Cambridge University Press, 2003), pp. 156–180.

If you're interested in the concept of quantum tunneling, you may wish to read Günter Nimtz and Astrid Haibel, *Zero Time Space: How Quantum Tunneling Broke the Light Speed Barrier* (New York: Wiley, 2008). The authors do a great job of describing this quantum phenomenon and relating it to the theory of relativity.

Percy Spencer's grandson, Rod Spencer, served as an invaluable resource for unearthing information about the inventor. You can read a

1958 *Reader's Digest* article about Percy's life at www.softslide.com/volumes/v2/t3/history/readers_digest.htm.

Elie Tahari's life story was featured in the Israeli newspaper *Haaretz* on July 16, 2009, in an article titled "The Man Who Dresses Angelina Jolie" by Raz Smolsky. You can find it (in the original Hebrew) at http://fashion.walla.co.il/?w=/2130/1520807. Tahari was also interviewed by *CBS Sunday Morning* on February 20, 2011. You can read the transcript of the story at http://www.cbsnews.com/stories/2011/02/20/sunday/main20034154.shtml.

Mardy Gilyard's touching account is chronicled in Pat Forde, "After Valleys, Gilyard Reaches Peak," December 30, 2009, http://sports.espn.go.com/ncf/bowls09/columns/story?columnist=forde_pat&id=4780034. You can learn even more about the story by reading Paul Daugherty, "Two Years After Being Homeless, Gilyard Has Cincy on Brink," December 2, 2009, http://sportsillustrated.cnn.com/2009/writers/paul_daugherty/12/02/mardy-gilyard/index.html.

All quotes from Stanford's dean of admission and financial aid, Richard Shaw, came from a 2007 talk he gave in Denver titled "Not Just a 4.0: An Insider's View of Stanford Admissions." It can be downloaded for free at iTunes U.

Chapter 2: The Limelight Effect

Julian Rotter's 1989 APA Award Address is "Internal Versus External Control of Reinforcement," *American Psychologist* 45 (1990): 489–493.

Rotter's original article about the differences between internal and external attribution styles was "Generalized Expectancies for Internal Versus External Control of Reinforcement," *Psychological Monographs: General & Applied* 80 (1966): 1–28.

The British longitudinal study that followed children into adulthood, measuring the effects of locus of control on health, is Catharine R. Gale, G. David Batty, and Ian J. Deary, "Locus of Control at Age 10 Years and Health Outcomes and Behaviors at Age 30 Years: The 1970 British Cohort Study," *Psychosomatic Medicine* 70 (2008): 397–403.

Robert C. Smolen and David A. Spiegel conducted the study that measured men's happiness in their relationship based on their locus of control. See Smolen and Spiegel, "Marital Locus of Control as a Modifier of the Relationship Between the Frequency of Provocation by Spouse and Marital Satisfaction," *Journal of Research in Personality* 21 (1987): 70–80.

Timothy A. Judge and Joyce E. Bono investigated the effects of locus of control on job satisfaction, compared with other psychological variables. See Judge and Bono, "Relationship of Core Self-

Evaluations Traits—Self-Esteem, Generalized Self-Efficacy, Locus of Control, and Emotional Stability—With Job Satisfaction and Job Performance: A Meta-Analysis," *Journal of Applied Psychology* 86 (2001): 80–92.

Two of the studies that indicate a relationship between entrepreneurs and an internal locus of control are Stanley Cromie and Sandra Johns, "Irish Entrepreneurs: Some Personal Characteristics," *Journal of Occupational Behaviour* 4 (1983): 317–324; and Robert H. Brokhaus, "Risk Taking Propensity of Entrepreneurs," *Academy of Management Journal* 23 (1980): 509–520.

Chapter 3: Meaning Making

You can read about the firsthand experiences of Major Rami Harpaz and the other captives in Amia Lieblich, *Seasons of Captivity* (New York: New York University Press, 1994).

J. Stuart Bunderson and Jeffery A. Thompson conducted the zookeeper study. See Bunderson and Thompson, "The Call of the Wild: Zookeepers, Callings, and the Double-Edged Sword of Deeply Meaningful Work," *Administrative Science Quarterly* 54 (2009): 32–57.

Robert N. Bellah, Richard Madsen, William M. Sullivan, Ann Swidler, and Steven M. Tipton, *Habits of the Heart: Individualism and Commitment in American Life* (Berkeley: University of California Press, 1996), discusses the notion of calling at work in chapter 3, "Finding Oneself."

To learn more about the benefits of a meaningful employment, read S. Antonio Ruiz-Quintanilla and George W. England, "How Working Is Defined: Structure and Stability," *Journal of Organizational Behavior* 17 (1996): 515–540; Rita Claes and S. Antonio Ruiz-Quintanilla, "Initial Career and Work Meanings in Seven European Countries," *Career Development Quarterly* 42 (1994): 291–301; Robert Knoop, "Work Values and Job Satisfaction," *The Journal of Psychology: Interdisciplinary and Applied* 128 (1994): 683–690; "The Relative Importance of Intrinsic and Extrinsic Rewards as Determinants of Work Satisfaction" by Clifford J. Mottaz, *The Sociological Quarterly* 26 (1985): 365–385; Bryan J. Dik and Ryan D. Duffy, "Calling and Vocation at Work: Definitions and Prospects for Research and Practice," *The Counseling Psychologist* 37 (2009): 424–450; and Michael F. Steger and Bryan J. Dik, "If One Is Looking for Meaning in Life, Does It Help to Find Meaning at Work?," *Applied Psychology: Health and Well-Being* 1 (2009): 303–320.

The link between meaning making and cognitive dementia is explored in Patricia A. Boyle, Aron S. Buchman, Lisa L. Barnes, and David A. Bennett, "Effect of a Purpose in Life on Risk of Incident: Alzheimer Disease and Mild Cognitive Impairment in Community-Dwelling Older Persons," *Archives of General Psychiatry* 67 (2010): 304–310.

Michael Steger's research about the power of meaning and the cross-cultural views on the search for meaning can be found in Michael F. Steger, Todd B. Kashdan, Brandon A. Sullivan, and Danielle Lorentz, "Understanding the Search for Meaning in Life: Personality, Cognitive Style, and the Dynamic Between Seeking and Experiencing Meaning," *Journal of Personality* 76 (2008): 199–228; and Michael F. Steger, Yoshito Kawabata, Satoshi Shimai, and Keiko Otake, "The Meaningful Life in Japan and the United States: Levels and Correlates of Meaning in Life," *Journal of Research in Personality* 42 (2007): 660–678.

Interpersonal interactions affect our subjective level of meaningfulness, as can be seen in Monisha Pasupathi and Ben Rich, "Inattentive Listening Undermines Self-Verification in Personal Storytelling," *Journal of Personality* 73 (2005): 1051–1086.

Chapter 4: Unwavering Commitment

Ruth Gordon, *An Open Book* (Garden City, N.Y.: Doubleday, 1980), tells the story of the actress's struggles to make it in the business.

Suzanne Kobasa's seminal research project about executives and their ability to cope with stress is described in Kobasa, "Stressful Life Events, Personality, and Health: An Inquiry into Hardiness," *Journal of Personality and Social Psychology* 37 (1979): 1–11.

To learn more about Paul Wellstone's political career, you can watch the DVD of *Wellstone!,* directed by Lu Lippold, Dan Luke, and Laurie Stern, 2005, Carry It Forward Productions. His two television advertisements, "Fast Paul" and "Looking for Rudy," are posted on YouTube.

Frederick Rhodewalt and Joan Zone authored "Appraisal of Life Change, Depression, and Illness in Hardy and Nonhardy Women," *Journal of Personality and Social Psychology* 56 (1989): 81–88.

Gordon Allport and H. S. Odbert conducted pioneering work on identifying core personality traits. See Allport and Odbert, "Trait-names: A Psycho-Lexical Study," *Psychological Monographs* 47 (1936).

Oddgeir Frieborg, Dag Barlaug, Monica Martinussen, Jan Rosenvinge, and Odin Hjemdal, "Resilience in Relation to Personality and Intelligence," *International Journal of Methods in Psychiatric Research* 14 (2005): 29–42, delineates the way in which various personality characteristics play a role in our ability to overcome adversity.

Chapter 5: Temperament and Success

The quotes from Kristin Schnake are taken from Graham Hays, "Schnake Brings Energy to Georgia Wins," May 31, 2009, http://sports.espn.go.com/ncaa/columns/story?columnist=hays_graham&id=4218602; and Laurence Conneff, "One Player's Loss Is

Another's Gain," *The Red and Black* (University of Georgia independent student newspaper), April 4, 2007.

Alexander Thomas and Stella Chess wrote about their longitudinal study of temperament in *Temperament and Development* (New York: Brunner/Mazel, 1977).

Quotes from John Donahoe are taken from his 2010 Stanford Graduate School of Business Spring Reunion Keynote address, "Leadership for Life." It can be viewed at http://www.youtube.com/watch?v=MBLmt6X0inU. You can learn more about John Donahoe's management style by reading David Gelles, "Easygoing Leader with a Devilish Smile," *Financial Times*, June 27, 2010, www.ft.com/cms/s/0/71293a78-80a1-11df-be5a-00144feabdc0.html#axzz1MN2YZC6Q.

Jan Smith and Margot Prior authored "Temperament and Stress Resilience in School-Age Children: A Within-Families Study," *Journal of the American Academy of Child and Adolescent Psychiatry* 34 (1995): 168–179.

Chapter 6: Humor Counteracting Adversity

The Allegheny humor and anxiety study is Nancy Yovetich, Alexander Dale, and Mary Hudak, "Benefits of Humor in Reduction of Threat-Induced Anxiety," *Psychological Reports* 66 (1990): 51–58.

Linda Henman's investigation of humor use by POWs is "Humor as a Coping Mechanism: Lessons from POWs," *International Journal of Humor Research* 14 (2001): 83–94.

The relationship among humor, resilience, and intelligence was examined by Ann Masten in "Humor and Competence in School-Aged Children," *Child Development* 57 (1986): 461–473.

Lorne Campbell, Rod Martin, and Jennie Ward investigated humor's role in relationship conflicts in "An Observational Study of Humor Use While Resolving Conflict in Dating Couples," *Personal Relationships* 15 (2008): 41–55.

Jenepher Lennox Terrion teamed up with Blake Ashforth to describe her observations of the officer training program in "From 'I' to 'We': The Role of Putdown Humor and Identity in the Development of a Temporary Group," *Human Relations* 55 (2002): 55–88.

Chapter 7: The Importance of a Satellite

Ellen A. Fagenson explored the beneficial effects of having a mentor in the workplace. Her research is detailed in "The Mentor Advantage: Perceived Career/Job Experiences of Proteges Versus Non-Proteges," *Journal of Organizational Behavior* 10 (1989): 309–320.

Jean Baldwin Grossman and Joseph P. Tierney teamed up to investigate the effects of the Big Brothers Big Sisters program on the young people it serves. See Grossman and Tierny, "Does Mentoring Work? An Impact Study of the Big Brothers Big Sisters Program," *Evaluation Review* 22 (1998): 403–426.

You can read more about Alice Goldberger's project working with children who survived the Holocaust in Sarah Moskowitz, *Love Despite Hate* (New York: Schocken Books, 1982).

Robin Pollock conducted research on the specific factors that contribute to the effectiveness of mentors. See Pollock, "A Test of Conceptual Models Depicting the Developmental Course of Informal Mentor-Protégé Relationships in the Work Place," *Journal of Vocational Behavior* 46 (1995): 144–162.

Acknowledgments

My favorite part of being an author involves the events that take place *after* a book gets published. After all the years of researching material, collecting stories, interviewing experts, and writing and re-writing drafts, I finally get to climb out of my writing cave and go on the road to speak in front of audiences. I get to connect with people, observing their reactions in real time—looking at their faces when they take in a story, laugh at a funny anecdote, or ask interesting questions.

This aspect of interacting with an audience got me curious about that dynamic. I interviewed Klaus Meine, the lead singer for the Scorpions, a hard-rock band that had performed for forty-five years before finally calling it quits in 2010. The Scorpions didn't just perform in easily accessible big-city venues; they trotted the globe, reaching as far as Siberia to get to their fans. "You feel the energy that comes from the audience," Meine explains. "And when it's that intense, you really can feel the magic."

According to Meine, performing live made him and his band-mates better musicians. "When you take the song out on the road," Meine says, "you find a different angle to it. Sometimes you even find ways to put in a different expression—even a strong expression.

And then to bring it to stage and play the song, many times it turns out that the live versions are even better than the recordings." You'd think that the opposite would be true. After all, in the studio musicians can record as many takes as needed, adjust the sound and vocals, and make sure the timing is just perfect. But something about the interaction with the audience brings out a creative energy that can't be replicated in a sterile studio.

Even for an author, there's something about the interaction with a live audience that takes the connection to a whole new level. In March 2011 I had the pleasure of speaking at Carl Sandburg College in Illinois (a shout-out to my gracious hosts, including Jill Johnson, Ken Grodjesk, Kelli Mayes-Denker, and Julie Gibb). Everyone at the event was welcoming, and the student audience was attentive and engaged. As I was speaking on stage, though, I couldn't help but notice two young attendees who sat in the front row. They looked slightly younger, and they were dressed more formally. But what really differentiated them from everyone else is that they asked a lot of good questions and it was obvious that they were deeply familiar with the material.

Just after my talk ended, as students approached the podium to ask questions and share their own personal stories and perspectives, one of the event coordinators introduced me to the two mystery audience members. I met Justin Weis and John Kemper and learned that they were actually high school students. Technically, they were skipping school to attend my talk. They had read *Sway* (which I co-authored with my brother, Ori) long before I was scheduled to come speak in Galesburg. When they saw a community announcement stating that I was going to appear in their small town, they couldn't quite believe it.

They obtained their parents' permission, arrived early so that they could grab good seats in the font, and dressed elegantly because they thought that's how college students would dress for a special event. They asked me to sign an event poster they had with them so that they could present it to their principal as proof that they hadn't just been cutting class.

It's always great to meet readers who enjoy the book, but what touched me most was when Justin and John told me that they hadn't been much into reading before they picked up *Sway*. The writing style resonated with them and got them engaged.

As an author, you don't often get to see the impact that your books have on people. I might walk past someone on the street who had just read one of my books, and neither of us would be the wiser. And with Justin and John, if it hadn't been for the coincidence that I spoke in their community, I would never have learned about how *Sway* had impacted their lives. Hearing that they enjoyed the book and that it turned them on to the world of reading is one of the greatest gifts an author could ask for.

To all of my readers who on some level connect with my books, even if we never get to meet—for me, knowing that there's that connection is the most meaningful part about writing. It's what helps inspire me.

One of the questions I'm often asked is about the process that leads up to the book. It starts with a vague concept that emerges in my head, a loosely formulated idea that I hope will one day coalesce into a book. Some topics don't survive for more than a few days. I come to the conclusion that there's not enough there or it's not quite interesting enough to pursue. They end up dissipating almost as fast as they were formed. Other ideas, though, stick around longer. If I think there might be something there, I bounce it around with my wife, Josyn, my parents, Tsilla and Hagay, my brother, Ori, and his wife, Hilary. I also appreciate the support and helpful suggestions I receive from my aunt Nira Chaikin, my great-aunt Sarah Zerkov, and my friends Rene Wong, Annie Shiau, Joe Pineda, Marco Gemignani, Boco Gutierrez, Edna "Mama" Smart, Steve Rotkoff, Judah Pollack, Amy Tedesco Pillitteri, Franz Epting, Alison Roberts, and the Lischinskys. Many of my psychological insights come from my work with the wonderful interns—past and present—whom I enjoy supervising and the terrific clients with whom I get to work.

Once I decide on a concept that is worthy of development, I run it by my spectacular agent, ICM's Esther Newberg. Esther has everything you'd want in an agent—drive, warmth, wit, spunk, and a genuine, heartfelt interest in people. Her entire team at ICM—Liz Farrell, Kari Stuart, Lyle Morgan—is the most professional, caring, and committed group of individuals you could ask for. They take customer service to a whole new level.

In today's ever-changing book publishing industry, it's rare for an author to work on three books—*Sway, Click,* and *Succeeding When You're Supposed to Fail*—with the same publisher. Roger Scholl and the team at Crown feel like family. The fact that my brother and I have continuously chosen to publish with them is testament to their great skill and the respect and dignity with which they treat their authors. Roger Scholl's suggestions and edits are fantastic. He has a gift for making anyone's writing sound smarter. Michael Palgon, Meredith McGinnis, Tara Gilbride, Talia Krohn, and Logan Balestrino all take great care of me and repeatedly go out of their way to be helpful.

I'm thankful for the patience and kindness I received from people who agreed to talk with me about their perspectives and experiences. Emmy Werner, an octogenarian, graciously offered to drive down to Palo Alto, if necessary, to meet me so we can talk about material for my book. Her enthusiasm about the topic of unlikely success is unparalleled. She kindly took me back in time to the earliest scientific investigations of people who overcame adversity. A few days after our conversation, I received copies of her articles that she had mailed me. They proved extremely helpful in my investigation.

Rod Spencer, Percy Spencer's grandson, takes after his grandfather with respect to intellectual curiosity and helpful spirit. He generously answered all my probing questions about his grandfather and shared with me all the material he has assembled over the years.

Michael Steger is patient, compassionate, and helpful. His insights into the nascent research area of meaning were invaluable. It's always a pleasure to meet an academic researcher who is so completely passionate about his topic of study.

David Underwood's inspiring story is a great example of the power of an easy temperament. Underwood painstakingly related to me the ordeal he had experienced, his approach to life's challenges, and his appreciation for everything that he has.

It's too bad that we can't somehow replicate Pablo Pazmiño. He's a fantastic surgeon, and he's equally adept at teaching. He's a true humanitarian who helps others whenever he can. Pazmiño's thoughtfulness, altruism, and devotion to improving the welfare of those who need assistance are inspiring.

And to all the other tunnelers out there who don't give up in the face of adversity, I hope your spirit remains strong.

Index